THE ENEMY IN THE MIRROR

THE ENEMY IN THE MIRROR

A Journey Worth Fighting For

By

Evangelist, Minister Constance D. Dixon,
BBA, MPA, MAEL

XULON PRESS

Xulon Press
2301 Lucien Way #415
Maitland, FL 32751
407.339.4217
www.xulonpress.com

xulon PRESS

© 2020 by Evangelist, Minister Constance D. Dixon, BBA, MPA, MAEL

All rights reserved solely by the author. The author guarantees all contents are original and do not infringe upon the legal rights of any other person or work. No part of this book may be reproduced in any form without the permission of the author. The views expressed in this book are not necessarily those of the publisher.

Unless otherwise indicated, Scripture quotations taken from the Holy Bible, New International Version (NIV). Copyright © 1973, 1978, 1984, 2011 by Biblica, Inc.™. Used by permission. All rights reserved.

Scripture quotations taken from the King James Version (KJV) – *public domain*.

Scripture quotations taken from the New American Standard Bible (NASB). Copyright © 1960, 1962, 1963, 1968, 1971, 1972, 1973, 1975, 1977, 1995 by The Lockman Foundation. Used by permission. All rights reserved.

Scripture quotations taken from the Holy Bible, New Living Translation (NLT). Copyright ©1996, 2004, 2007 by Tyndale House Foundation. Used by permission of Tyndale House Publishers, Inc.

Printed in the United States of America.

Paperback ISBN-13: 978-1-6312-9939-1
eBook ISBN-13: 978-1-6312-9940-7

"I will praise thee; for I am fearfully and wonderfully made: marvelous are thy works; and that my soul knoweth right well" (Ps. 139:14).

This book is dedicated:

To my loving husband, Richard. in whom I thank and praise God for being my lord and king. As the scripture states in Proverbs 18:22 *"Whoever finds a wife finds a good thing and obtains favor of Yahweh."*

To my parents whom I love dearly, thank you for your nurturing, love, and confidence in my God-given abilities.

To my friends who are few, keep fighting the good fight of faith.

To my children whom I have watched and nurtured through the power of God Almighty, stay focus, and continue to say <u>**yes**</u> to God's perfect way.

To the many of you who've played a significant role throughout my life's journey; I thank you.

And most of all, more than life itself, I thank God Almighty, God the Son, and God the Holy Ghost for the direction as I progress through my life of trials and tribulation, for the love which brought me out, and for the blood that gave me life and that more abundantly. What more can I give but <u>**my reasonable service?**</u> *"I beseech you therefore, brethren, by the mercies of God, that ye present your bodies a living sacrifice, holy, acceptable unto God, which is your reasonable service. And be not conformed to this world: but be ye transformed by the renewing of your mind, that ye may prove what is that good, and acceptable, and perfect, will of God" (Rom, 12:1-2 KJV).* **I give** <u>**my life.**</u>

Finally, I dedicate this second book in a series to all of you who have made my living, not in vain.

SPEAK LORD, SPEAK!

Foreword

My previous book, *How Can I Escape*, gives credence to life's struggles, problems, and hardships every person experiences. Moreover, it concludes the reality of finding one's path and knowing God is the administrator of our life. The battle in finding your path does not supersede the greater importance of having a relationship with Christ who can and will make a way, not for you, not just to escape but to live victorious through every situation, every circumstance, and every problem. Even though there is a continuous desire to seek avenues, routes, and paths as short cuts to relieve the hardships and pains that life in general hands out, we must stay true to the journey that is before us. It is not about whether we escape our difficulties, but rather to understand that Christ is the only answer to our transformation from the present works of darkness into His present world of solace and harmony unto obedience. (His present world is "kosmos" which in Greek means "God's orderly arrangement.")

Escaping is not a mere allusion of thought, deed, or mind; it is a reality of who and what Christ is. He is not based on mere allusion but in fact through the undeniable faith of God. Again, and I stress, just agree with God and you will see for yourself that in Christ we can truly escape both physically and spiritually. Does this mean we will not encounter some type of discomfort on this journey to know and become who Christ will have us to be? Are our struggles, our hardships, and our problems here to destroy? Are they to build, hinder, or to nurture? Yes and no. To destroy the working of the flesh—yes! To hinder— no! To build—yes! To nurture—yes!

Truly the response or the action that one takes is based upon whether our enemy-flesh is placed under subjection to the perfect and unadulterated word of God. Therefore, while escaping, we see that we cannot escape in our hearts, mind, or soul until we say yes to God's will and understand with whom we fight and struggle. *The Enemy in the Mirror* uncovers the spiritual battle with **self**. I pray you will recognize and understand your flesh as well as recognize and understand your significant role in the cross. Seek the Lord now; seek His face daily; crucify and deny your nature, and be blessed.

Lord, I surrender my life unto the Alpha and the Omega, the beginning and the end, the balm of my soul. Jesus come in and sup with me as I sup with you. Teach me your ways that I may not stray, teach me your love that I may represent you as you love me, teach me to hope that I may see faith in all that you do in my life and in every life you allow me to touch. Deliver me from evil and deliver me from my self-centered ways, and fill me more and more with your embodied love. Cause my flesh to die that you may live in me daily. In this I pray and believe.... AMEN

Table of Contents

Foreword..vii

1. A Spiritual Journey...................................1
2. The Violent Taketh it by Force.......................17
3. Nature of Sin–The Beast and Falling into Ritualism.....28
4. Deception...50
5. If the Law of God Is Terrible, Then What Breaks It?.....67
6. The Call..78
7. Deceptive Faith and Counterfeit Works...............83
8. Trying to Be Somebody in a Nobody's Dead Church....99
9. What Does Love Have to Do with It?.................115
10. I Must Surrender..................................121
11. A Physical Only Abstinence Mindset................133
12. Manifestations of an Evil Nature...................146
13. How Can I Escape?................................154
14. The State of Man..................................179
15. Spiritual Discipline vs. Addictions..................186
16. Freedom from Bondage............................192
17. My House...198
18. Judging—Who Me?................................212
19. Counterfeit Religion: The Changing Times and Laws...223
20. What Should I Do?................................228

Epilogue: Personal Reflection..........................230
References..233

Chapter 1

A Spiritual Journey

Cold, uninhibited thoughts of yesteryears grip my mind as I gazed out of my window. I found myself yearning and desiring God to deliver me from this bondage, bondage that lay so heavily on my mind as though one had placed it around my neck as a sarsen. This bondage—death to self—was a familiar partner; a friend of some sort, a nuisance of the kind no one wants to have in their presence.

However, as I stared into the open skies, I sensed the promise, the anticipation, the expectancy of what I believe faith to be. I began to reach towards this hope which appeared to me like a balloon flying effortlessly in the wind waiting for some passerby to reach up and grab its lissome string. I stood, expecting the calm before the raging storm, yet with disbelief I sighed, reaching a point perhaps of no return, my heart becoming heavy as even the beats itself faded into a melancholy blues rhapsody. Shaking myself, I saw I could grasp for the blessed hope in knowing that His will is what I seek, that I could knock and hope the door would open, that I would find the blessed Savior, The Hope of Glory, who will never forsake nor dismiss me. Oh, how sweet to know Him, to know truly the love He has for me, a love that hides a multitude of faults, sins, failures, and disappointments, is a love that surpasses all eternities and understanding. That His love is brought forth as pure gold to the suffering, the sacrifice, the death, and His resurrection.

Trials and tribulations, loss of a job, loss of my natural father and now being plagued with skin cancer. This place and time of lonesomeness had brought me to my knees, crying out for this trial, this cup, to pass me by. Yet during this storm, the raging reciprocals of drops that pound against the mind of perception engulfed me. It portrayed itself as a whip fitted for the destruction of my flesh. The torment and pain, despair and impossibilities, loss and abandoned dreams, pressed upon my broken and shattered heart. I felt this piercing and throbbing weight of force as a neurosis of my mind, dragging me against my will of self-want, self-desires, and self-exaltation. I heard, *"If any of you wants to be my follower, you must turn from your selfish ways, take up your cross, and follow me"* (Matt. 16:24 NLT).

I wished it was easy. I asked, "Why can't I die to my affections? Why do I place so much importance on myself?" Yet I heard in the deepness of my soul I must die. "Father," – I cried out, "forgive me for my unbelief, forgive me for my selfishness. Lord Jesus, rescue your child; My Father, rescue me from me."

As I continued to attack my flesh from within, my focus shifted to the hills afar off. They offered the structure of strength I have known for many years. From this mountain, this foundation from where my help comes from, I find my stability, my rock, my assurance in the time of trouble. "Jesus, my Master, and Lord," I begin, yet I struggle to keep my focus. Amnesia, temporary collapse of doubt, causes me to stray from the remnant of God's immeasurable love and its comfort. *"Whoever dwells in the shelter of the Most High will rest in the shadow of the Almighty. I will say of the Lord, He is my refuge and my fortress, my God, in whom I trust"* (Ps. 91:1-2 NIV).

Oh, how I yearned at that moment for the immediate embrace, the concept of love, the certain obedience of the mountains, the encirclement of God's perfect and complete love for His creation. Do you see how they hold firm to faith, hope, and the stability of trust that portrays our Heavenly Father. These mountains hold their position, never calling out in desperation, never calling out in fear, yet– even when pieces begin to crumble and fall and when time and erosion have bombarded their mysteries.

My soul cried out with a lament of sorrow, "my God." But the tears I hoped would fall do not escape my eyes. The shout comes from within, the call as a helpless child; is there no balm in my soul. Will there be one? Will I know a good Samaritan to walk across my path, to stop and lend me a helping hand? I cry out to the All-Knowing God, "How long, oh Majestic God, how long will thou not answer your child? How long will I be broken and estranged from my Living Maker, the Lover of my soul? Help, Lord Jesus, help."

The wretchedness was heavier than it had been before. The mind-boggling thoughts of self-destruction and despondency had directed me to this land, this place of loathsome where I cried out from the pits of hell and destruction but heard no resolve.

The dragging of my soul, the exacerbation, the exhaustion.... will someone please help me for I've fallen and have no desire to get up? I felt limp, lethargic, and apathetic to any sign of relief, living spiritually drained. I found fragments of judgments, opinions, viewpoints, traditions, and rituals bombarding my concept of reality unto a fraction of perception, a destroyed state almost in ruins.

I was silently manifesting itself into gluttony of all means (lust of the eyes), self-love (lust of the flesh), and self-addiction in all forms (pride of life), which soon aligned itself as sin, transgression, and estrangement from the Almighty, Everlasting God of my soul. As I sat discussing within myself this volatile account, hoping even those who called themselves friends would understand this destruction, this beast that had taken the bountifulness of God's mercy and grace and laid it before me like a noose fitted for my demise. Lies, perception, and failures outlined the wantonness of yesterday's beliefs and dreams; hatred and misunderstandings perpetuated propaganda as a covering headpiece, the armor once was vibrant and alive was now distant and inhibited. Self- hatred wore its garment of strife and sedition. *"Beware lest any man spoils you through philosophy and vain deceit, after the tradition of men, after the rudiments of the world, and not after Christ"* (Col. 2:8).

Accusations and judgments continued to cloud my mind as I sought a balm to ease my weary and troubled soul. Thoughts of depression pursued me as a baby yearns for its mother's milk. Despondency and despair, the vestment of covetousness, draped itself upon my shoulders forcing each bone to succumb to the pressure of life exposing the very existence of death to self. This beast ramping throughout myself abducted the very thought and process of faith in the God of my soul.

This self-destructing behavior was overthrowing the perfect and complete will of God the Father; in this I understand, in this, I have the knowledge and the ability to escape, but I do not want to run, hide, nor escape the pruning of my fleshly desires of self-want, self-righteousness, and the "I'm alright" syndrome. The breaking of my fallow ground and letting the will of God Almighty take its authority in my life will deliver me to the life of victory and obedience as a true believer, achiever, and conqueror. As I pondered, I still found myself mired in a place where pain and frustration had taken control of my very being, succumbing to the authority of fear so that I wore this beast as a garb of doubt and anguish. Oh, how I had allowed the enemy to use my emotions, my thoughts, and even my actions. As I turn slowly back to the mountains where I once found solace, my flesh cried out, "Father, rescue me from ME! For here I stand, for here I lie in the waddling of despair; I ask who is this beast, this enemy in my mirror? How can I escape?"

Have you been there? Have you ever had thoughts of defeat through your trials and tribulations?

Today, I want to express something so drastic that if it could be shouted from every mountaintop to the pulpits of your soul, it would be of relief to all calamity of self-annihilation. Yet, as I speak and sound the trumpet today, the enemy is bringing forth obliteration on the natural and spiritual lives within God's orderly arrangement—Christianity—as I know and understand today. Self-destruction is an instrument the enemy uses with our flesh to kill, steal, and destroy our victory in God Almighty and strip us of our pure relationship with Him This tool of ignorance, desperation, and hopelessness has been used through the ages by the workers of darkness, by satan himself as an open attack upon our Christian belief system.

I am reminded of the Psalmist as he spoke of Israel's desperation. Israel firmly believed God was a God of life, a God who frees from oppression. However, the people of God repeatedly forgot the power of God's love and how He delivered His people through natural causes, judges, wars, and even pestilence. Just as the children of Israel then, we today take on the same persona as we continue to mark our understanding of the True and Living God based on what we can get from Him. There are times when we feel we don't belong or we have such a strong need of acceptance that we would give our souls to those we feel we have to be accepted by.

Yet, it will come to a time when we will have to stand strong through adversities, problems, hatred, and the maleficent actions of others. Psalm 22 shows such a stand of faith through adversity and strife, even when others mock your faithfulness to God, know it is trust in God that the scoffers are trying to undermine. In this Psalm, the expression of *lament* the Psalmist expresses is not based on solely feelings or emotions but that he **believes and trusts** that God does care and is always within crying distance. Lamenting is not a failure of faith but an act of faith.

Sometimes it may seem from our human perspective that God is far away and the enemy is very near. You cry out to God. You cannot take any more of the pressure from every side, the torment and anguish that takes a toll upon your body and mind causing physical and psychological breakdown and even longing for death. It is when the constant attacks of the enemy's devices emerge from his workers of darkness and wickedness that an outburst of desperation comes from within your uttermost being, *"Lord, Lord, why has thou forsaken me"* (Ps. 22:1). Yet here is the struggle and war with oneself—to finally give way to thinking that all is lost; that anxiety, grief, and fear will forever grip the soul. But the cry out for God was expressed—the cry of one who suffers innocently, of one who is surrounded by an enemy and mocked precisely because of his faithfulness, devotion, and commitment. God rescues! God hears the cry of the afflicted and brings deliverance to the cry of His child. This short lamentation, *"Lord, Lord, why has thou forsaken me"* was an offering of praise, adoration, and worship to God Almighty (Ps. 22:1). God will never forsake or leave you. We are just as a child lost in a crowded mall crying out for his /her parents to rescue him when we, as God's children, cry out to the One who will rescue us from ourselves and every damnable thing that would come up against us.

When we value our substance as being as being the all of all means, we will never reach the pinnacle of happiness or hope which is the Victorious Life of Abundance. Basing who and what we are on another's ideology and attempting to mold ourselves into their lifestyle, their desires, and dreams will leave us unfulfilled. That is when we become despondent, unsatisfied, unsympathetic, and hopeless. Unwilling to move from this self-defeated attitude, we cry out that we are "righteous" as we stand in the despairing pit of disobedience, showing forth all forms of hatred to the temple (your body) that houses the Holy Ghost, that implementer of the Son, Jesus Christ. Consider the enemy in the mirror. Time after time we choose to see everyone as the problem instead of seeing who the true culprit is. We blame coworkers, parents, friends, our community, the government, and the list goes on. Whether someone or something has helped initiate our fall, our pain, or our troubles, it doesn't matter; if we begin to look into our image, make-up, and self-deception we will find that the fault lies within our character, our flesh, our nature from the beginning.

Sometimes we become so deceitful that we cloud our judgment with hallucinations, mirages, and feelings against people for no apparent reason. These thoughts and actions outlined by our attitudes and jealousy, perceptions, and ideas, cause us to respond in guile and a deceitful way. We believe our conjured up lies before we acknowledge the truth.

As these thoughts of delusion persist and continue in our prideful mode, we seek positions and people where we can showcase our flesh of talents, our flesh of desires, and our flesh of wants with an explosion of maliciousness to our inner man which is Christ the Hope of Glory. When we fail to reach a certain plateau in our lives, we begin to point fingers at everyone we possibly can think of to stop the attack of our inadequate thoughts (my mother left me, my father was not there, I don't know my father, I was rape, I was sodomized, etc.). It is not to say these things are not hurtful to one's natural growth; however, to belabor or prolong being in this pool of inadequacies only destroys the life and victory that God Almighty has outlined for you. Scripture clearly states if you are for Jesus,

> "'No weapon formed against you shall prosper, and every tongue which rises against you n judgment You shall condemn. This is the heritage of the servants of the LORD, and their righteousness is from Me,' Says the LORD" (Isa. 54:17 NKJV).

Or how about,

> "What shall we then say to these things? If God be for us, who can be against us?" (Rom. 8:31 KJV).

I do understand that even in this state of apostasy (falling away from the truth), some, no matter what transpires, will make excuses and point the finger at others saying it is their fault. However, I ask, how many times do we give our mind, body, soul, spirit, and self-worth to the highest bidder so that we can be accepted, loved, and adorned or be a part of the world's agenda? We strive continuously for this type of a toxic relationship that feeds our lust for self-greed to no immediate satisfaction. We commit to the lewdness of thought and action. This lack of decorum walks hand in hand with satan and your flesh to castrate the unfeigned love of God, causing you to become numb, wanton, and unconstrained. Scripture states:

> "Do not let any part of your body become an instrument of evil to serve sin. Instead, give yourselves completely to God, for you were dead, but now you have new life. So use your whole body as an instrument to do what is right for the glory of God" (Rom.6:13 NLT 2007).

And still, some will take the defense of "it wasn't my fault" or "it's nothing wrong with me", not recognizing they need to be rescued from a life of self-hatred. Self-hatred is not a reason to *give oneself* over to sin; this means your members (feet, hands, thoughts, tongue, body, mind, and soul) to Satan. Again, the Scriptures state:

> *"Know ye not, that to whom ye yield yourselves servants to obey, his servants ye are to whom ye obey; whether of sin unto death, or of obedience unto righteousness?"* (Rom. 6:16 KJV).

> *"Put to death, therefore, whatever belongs to your earthly nature: sexual immorality, impurity, lust, evil desires and greed, which is idolatry"* (Col. 3:5 NIV).

The enemy in the mirror has lived its life for me, myself, and I—the Self. I dare not say satan did not initiate the attack, however; there are some things your flesh wants to do, enjoys doing, and desires to do. This we need to own up to it so we may be delivered. Now in no way is this a condemnation because of what has happened to you on your journey to where you are now. If you continue to hold onto the negative baggage and allow words and things to take precedent over your life, your thoughts, and action you will in no wise grow or achieve the things that have been purposed for you by God. In His word He states:

> *"But as for you, ye thought evil against me; but God meant it unto good, to bring to pass, as it is this day, to save much people alive"* (Gen 50:20).

Therefore, look at it from a time continuum. You are still here and God wants you to see Him for who He is, and that's as your DELIVERER, SAVIOR, MASTER, and LORD; your, I AM, THAT I AM (Exod. 3:14).

You could ask, "If it's that simple then why do I continue to fall into this trap of depression, despondency, and despair whether it is the indulgence of the flesh or not?" You could continue to ask, "Why do I feel the way I feel and do the things I do? And why, after doing and feeling this way, do I become bitter, contentious, and un-forgiven which I know will lead to a life of unfulfilled promises"

As I reflected on my periods of rebellion, I heard the 3 D's— despondency, despair, and depression— ringing like sounding brass, permeating through my mind I could not help to sigh and reflect upon the strength that God Almighty has given unto me during my battles of self-hatred. Reflecting on the restoration that has taken a hold of my very soul, I remember looking for a sign of hope, a testament of faith, and even asked where is the "so greater cloud of witnesses" that once were my abettor? Finally, with nothing left in me, I surrendered unto my destiny as so you must accede to your destined place as a chosen vessel, fitted and shaped for the Master's use. Therefore, the answer is that many refused to surrender to the powerful hand of God – to be of His good purpose which is our reasonable service (Rom. 12:1c KJV). Normally, we move before we are told but some never move and sit waiting for the call unto Repentance and Salvation, that sincere milk of God's Holy Word who is Jesus wrapped into all that we need and desire.

Let us look at another example. 1 Samuel 16:1 gives us the prelude to David's life as the youngest son of Jesse.

David started as a shepherd and a musician. In David's duty, he cared and faithfully looked after the sheep until one day a bear came into the sheepfold and caught a little lamb. David heard the lamb's cry, however, and ran after the bear. When he caught it, he took the lamb out of the beast's mouth and smote the bear. In another instance, a lion came into the fold and stole a sheep from out of the flock. David went out and found the lion with the sheep still in its mouth. He grabbed the lion by the beard and smote it as well. He killed the lion and delivered the lamb safely. During this same period, King Saul became sick and was tormented by an evil spirit. Saul sent messengers to Jesse requesting David to come and play his harp for the king. The sound of the harp was soothing and thus David found **favor** with Saul as he played his music. King Saul was restored, the evil spirit departed from him, and David became the chief musician and armor bearer for the king.

Now, 1st Samuel 17 states, while during the reign of King Saul, the Philistine army gathered in the land of Judah to make war on the Israelites. The army set up camp on a hill overlooking the Valley of Elah while the Israelites under Saul camped on the opposite hill. Goliath positioned himself between the two armies and challenged the Israelites to send out a warrior to meet him in single combat. If the Israelite champion prevailed, the Philistines would become the subjects of Saul. If Goliath won, then the Israelites would become slaves unto the Philistines.

For forty days, in both the morning and evening, Goliath issued his challenge, taunting the Israelites and insulting their True and Living God. No man came forward to meet him except one—David. When delivering food to his brothers on the battlefield, David heard Goliath's haughty challenge and burned with anger. The youth came to Saul and offered to fight the giant. Though initially skeptical of David's capacity to defeat Goliath, Saul was persuaded to allow the match after the young Bethlehemite detailed his previous victorious encounters with a bear and a lion.

Just think: if he did not have the preparation, the trials, and the tribulation, would David have been ready for his promotion from God?

David rejected the king's offer of armor and a sword and went out to fight Goliath with only a staff, sling, and five smooth stones he had taken from a nearby stream. Goliath sent his shield-bearer before him, moving slowly closer to the Israelite champion. Seeing that he was in reality only a boy, Goliath took his presence as an insult, believing that the Israelites must send out the mightiest warrior to meet him. Goliath responded: *"Am I a dog, that you come at me with sticks?"* (1 Sam. 17:43). Goliath cursed David by his gods, and taunted:

> *Come here and I'll give your flesh to the birds of the air and the beasts of the field!" In the battle of words, his young opponent (David) proved to be a worthy one, retorting: "You come against me with sword and spear and javelin, but I come against you in the Name of the Lord Almighty, the God of the armies of Israel, whom you have defied... Today I will give the carcasses of the Philistine army to the birds of the air and the beasts of the earth, and the whole world will know that there is a God in Israel."* 1Samuel 17:44-46

Hearing enough, Goliath closed in to attack. David ran quickly toward the battle line to meet him. Reaching into his bag and taking out a stone, he slung it and struck Goliath on the forehead. Before the mighty Philistine could even attempt a blow, the stone sank into Goliath's forehead and he collapsed face down on the ground. David then drew Goliath's sword from its scabbard and cut off his head (1 Sam. 17:47-58). What victory by the hand of God through a shepherd boy who was willing to surrender his heart, mind, and body to the God of his soul, regardless of the obstacles and fears he faced.

> *"For God hath not given us the spirit of fear; but of power, and of love, and of a sound mind"* (2 Tim 1:7 KJV).

Here David, a mighty warrior, musician, worshipper, murderer, and adulterer, was known as a *"man after God's own heart"* (1 Sam. 13:13-15) who was called by God to deliver Judah and Israel. From his birth on, David was predestined, chosen by God to do His good purpose. Yes, even an adulterer and a murderer can be called a "man after God's own heart." So, in reality, there is no excuse—no matter what you have done, stated, and relayed—that will cease the love of God from coming into your life. Why? Because when David failed, or even when we fail, we must repent and turn back to God. As the Scripture states:

> *"If my people, which are called by my name, shall humble themselves, and pray, and seek my face, and turn from their wicked ways; then will I hear from heaven, and will forgive their sin, and will heal their land"* (2 Chron 7:14 KJV).

> *Have mercy upon me, O God, according to thy lovingkindness: according unto the multitude of thy tender mercies blot out my transgressions. Wash me thoroughly from mine iniquity, and cleanse me from my sin. For I acknowledge my transgressions: and my sin is ever before me. Against thee, thee only, have I sinned, and done this evil in thy sight: that thou mightest*

be justified when thou speakest, and be clear when thou judgest.

Behold, I was shapen in iniquity; and in sin did my mother conceive me. Behold, thou desirest truth in the inward parts: and in the hidden part thou shalt make me to know wisdom. Purge me with hyssop, and I shall be clean: wash me, and I shall be whiter than snow. Make me to hear joy and gladness; that the bones which thou hast broken may rejoice. Hide thy face from my sins, and blot out all mine iniquities. Create in me a clean heart, O God; and renew a right spirit within me. Cast me not away from thy presence; and take not thy holy spirit from me. Restore unto me the joy of thy salvation; and uphold me with thy free spirit. Then will I teach transgressors thy ways; and sinners shall be converted unto thee. Deliver me from bloodguiltiness, O God, thou God of my salvation: and my tongue shall sing aloud of thy righteousness. O Lord, open thou my lips; and my mouth shall shew forth thy praise. For thou desirest not sacrifice; else would I give it: thou delightest not in burnt offering. The sacrifices of God are a broken spirit: a broken and a contrite heart, O God, thou wilt not despise. Do good in thy good pleasure unto Zion: build thou the walls of Jerusalem. Then shalt thou be pleased with the sacrifices of righteousness, with burnt offering and whole burnt offering: then shall they offer bullocks upon thine altar. Psalm 51 KJV

I am also reminded of David's victory and strength as a valiant commander in war, turning within to the authority and power that gave him strength and victory. He encouraged himself in the Lord when all oppositions set forth to destroy him, to seduce and overthrow the authority in his life (1 Sam. 30:8). You can see this in how his fellow soldiers who fought side-by-side in battles with him and shared fellowship wanted to stone him due to what they considered a defeat. The army had just conquered a nation and while returning home to celebrate the victory they discovered their wives, children, and the elderly had been taken captive by the Amalekites and their city had been burned down. David's men wanted to stone him due to the shock, anxiety, and frustration of having lost their families and possessions. His fellow brethren wanted to stone David to death and destroy him.

At that moment, the men allowed their flesh and their emotions to take control of them. They forgot who they served and that they had a victory by the hand of their king. Did they not think David was perplexed as well as his wife, children, and kindred were in the number and his possessions were destroyed and burned also?

David readily requested for the ephod (garment of clothing) and began to require of God Almighty his trust. His alignment of thought, action, and deed rested in the true and living God. He caught hold of himself, keeping from going mad from rage, anger, and frustration and bowing to the mighty hand of God, the restorer of one's soul, the deliverer, the captain of his life. David submitted humbly to the hand of God for guidance, leadership, and direction. Thinking over whether he should pursue, he encourages himself instead of the God of War, God of his Salvation, his Redeemer, and Savior. David succumbed to the Anointing of God and asked, *"Shall I pursue my enemy?"* The Lord stated, *"pursue thy enemy and thou shall recover all"* (1 Sam. 30 KJV). What a victory David obtained! His army defeated the enemy outside of the camp, recovered their family and kindred, and received more than what they had anticipated. What a powerful God we serve.

Can you not hear wisdom in this? Can you not accept this wisdom at this moment within the black hole of the galaxy of your soul? Can you now submit unto the awesomeness and splendor of the power of God?

Here is wisdom. When those who stand by the wayside waiting to discourage, to breakdown, to destroy, and to kill (Satan's imps, demons, and workers of iniquity), we must be vigilant and say *"…..for the battle is the LORD'S, and he will give you into our hands"* (1 Sam. 17:47). Yes, even when it seems as if hell—Satan, himself, and a host of fallen angels— begin to attack, though the very thought and veracity of the Living God who operates in your life from every avenue that you move and function withing, you must remember the *"violent taketh it by force"* (Matt. 11:12).

Chapter 2

THE VIOLENT TAKETH IT BY FORCE

Let's look at this deeper the phrase "the violent taketh it by force." First, the Old Testament is divided into three parts: the law, the prophets, and the writings. Jesus uses two of the portions to make a point; the *prophets* and the *law* pointed to the Messiah.

John is the last of the Old Testament prophets. By rejecting John's message, the scribes and/or the religious authorities rejected the witness of the Scriptures (John 5:39). The prophets spoke of who He is and what He would do. The phrase *"the kingdom of heaven suffers violence"* refers to how religious men used positions of authority to bully their way into control of the religious institution of Christ's time. John the Baptist also challenged the status quo of the religious leaders of his day, which was the Jewish synagogue, but, more particularly, the Jewish temple with its wealth, rituals, customs, and practices as well as its prestige and status as a political establishment. These religious leaders of his day, the. Pharisees and the Sadducees were holding the people captive by their made-up laws and reacted strongly to John's message. Instead of obeying him, they tried to hold their positions of authority. Can you see this same legalism today?

The original Greek word "biázœ" (Mickelson Strong's Concordance 2015) in Matthew 11:12 is translated as "suffers violence". Biázœ is a compound word originating from a root "bias" (Mickelson Strong's Concordance 2015) meaning strength. Biázœ means literally *"to overpower by rushing forcefully into.*

In Matthew 11:12, "biázetai" is used in the present indicative passive but also used with middle voice (for self-interests) (Riggenmann 2018). Present indicative affirms *something that is occurring while the speaker (Jesus) is making his statement*; passive voice shows the subject (the kingdom of God) as *receiving the action* (i.e. forceful violence) of the verb; the middle voice indicates the subject as acting in some way upon himself or concerning himself (i.e., the violent force their way into the kingdom for their interests, not God's).

> *"Repent, for the kingdom of heaven is at hand!"*
> (Matt. 3:20)

The kingdom suffered violence from the religious despots (authoritarians) who did not want to relinquish their control to the message of John the Baptist that the Messiah was coming.

> *"But when he saw many of the Pharisees and Sadducees come to his baptism, he said unto them, 'O generation of vipers, who hath warned you to flee from the wrath to come'"* (Matt. 3:7 KJV)

Violence is not how one enters the kingdom but with humility and meekness as those who desire to do so humble themselves as sinners and repent. But the religious leaders did not repent from John's preaching to prepare themselves for the one who was to come (John 1:6-8; Luke 7:28-30).

> *"But woe to you, scribes and Pharisees, hypocrites! For you shut up the kingdom of heaven against men; for you neither go in yourselves nor do you allow those who are entering to go in* (Matt. 23:13).

This is a scary thought when you consider that. just as in the days of John the Baptist, today there are self-righteous and religious folks forcing their way on others. Pastors, ministers, tele-evangelists, false teachers, and false prophets use the church pulpit and ecclesiastical positions to acquire wealth and power. Instead of being shepherds who feed God's sheep, their very existence as paid ministers is done for their livelihood.

The violence today can be found in the self-righteous attitude of religious men who fail to recognize the day of their visitation and who exercise violence towards the kingdom of God (i.e., believers proclaiming the truth). The context first reveals itself when John the Baptist arrived on the scene for public ministry. He did not come in finely dressed clothing or with softly spoken words to tickle one's ears. John the Baptist *"had his raiment of camel's hair, and leather girdle about his loins; and his meat was locust and wild honey"* (Matt. 3:4 KJV). He was a rough and tumble looking character who came out from the arid Judean wilderness declaring that everyone in every place should repent.

John's message created opposition in all points, making waves within the confines of the self-righteous mindset. The hypocritical sects of the Pharisees and Sadducees had controlled the minds and money of the masses of Jews for many years under the sanction of Rome, and they had been strengthened politically by the recent appointment of Herod who believed he was a Jew and the true ruler of the Jews. Herod respected John greatly but he also played the political role to appease the Jewish rulers because they held sway with the people.

Then came this man who did not look the part, did not act the part of a religious ruler, who did not have the physical nor material influences and status as the religious leaders. John in his persona spared no one, and even Herod himself was told to repent for his adulterous affair with his brother's wife. Herold was told to repent by John, which ended up landing John into prison. The response to John's message was the violence spoken of by Jesus in Matthew 11:12. The Jews accused John of having a demon. This type of verbal accusation was a form of violence. It was the wrathful hatred of a sect of jealous hypocrites. They were Satan's children, and their nature was the same as that of the devil...violent.

After John was imprisoned, Herod's wife, Herodias, who was infuriated by John's condemnation of her marriage demanded that Herod cut off his head and have it publicly displayed on a platter. Therefore, as Jesus said, *"And from the days of John the Baptist until now the kingdom of heaven suffers violence"* (Matthew 11:12).

What does the phrase "violent men take it by force" mean?

The phrase in the second half of Matthew 11:12 reads, *"and violent men take it by force."* The Greek word translated as "take it by force" is "harpázousin." (Thayer 2017, G726) This Greek verb connotes seizing or grasping something with speed and force. The Jews forced their way into the ministry of John the Baptist, but he would have none of their antics. When John publicly rebuked Herod for his adultery, Herod's violent reaction was to have John seized by force and imprisoned.

- *"violent men"* – *(Thayer 2017) biastês; from (*Mickelson Strong's Concordance 2015*); a forcer, i.e. (figuratively) energetic*

- *"take by force"*–*(Mickelson Strong's Concordance 2015) harpazo; from a derivative of (Thayer 2017); to seize (in various applications): Harpazo comes from a root Greek word, haireomai (Thayer 2017) which means, "to take for oneself, i.e. to prefer"*

The Greek definitions above mean Matthew 11:12 can be translated as follows, *"and men who act as forcers seize them by force."* (Bluemel 2007). This is exactly what happened to John the Baptist and Jesus Christ; they were both seized and taken by force. John was seized and thrown into prison only to be beheaded later. Jesus was seized in the garden of Gethsemane and tried and crucified.

In Christian churches today, many ministers and pastors are guilty of lording over their flocks. They rule the roost with severity and domination. They want to control the logical and thinking people among their congregations by not allowing any public discussion of or disagreement with their teaching. In this manner, self-made ecclesiastical tyrannical rulers are causing violence to the kingdom of God (i.e., God's flock). With force, they seize upon the minds and wallets of the church members, breaking them down physically and mentally to where there is no mindset to stand and resist (this is great brainwashing at its best).

The Concordant Literal New Testament (below) provides a much more accurate translation of Matthew 11:12 and the related context in Luke 16:16.

- *Matthew 11:12: "Now, from the days of John the Baptist hitherto, the kingdom of the heavens is being violently forced and the violent are snatching it."*

- *Luke 16:16 "The law and the prophets are unto John; thenceforth, the evangel of the kingdom of God is being brought, and everyone is violently forcing into it, and the violent are snatching it. Yet it is easier for heaven and earth to pass by than for one serif of the law to fall."*

The parallel gospel in Luke 16:13-17 gives a greater interpretation concerning the violence. In that passage, Jesus is talking to the Pharisees, not to those who truly seek the truth. The Pharisees prided themselves on the knowing Law and the Prophets, but now that the kingdom of God was being preached (first by John, then by Jesus), the Jews want to force their way into it. One method they frequently used to exercise violence against Jesus was scoffing at him. They did this in an attempt to discredit him through ridicule. Can you see this happening today in Christendom?

Two facts stand out most in this text. First, the Pharisees were "lovers of money," and this helps define Jesus's use of "biazo" to describe the "bias" meaning "of life, they were living". Second, the Pharisees were those who justified themselves in the sight of men; this shows how they were forcing their way into the kingdom. Seeking to please men by an outward show of righteousness, the Pharisees operated like a pack of wolves in sheep's clothing using their position as spiritual leaders to capitalize on the naïve and ignorant.

Jesus illustrates how the Pharisees used their power to accumulate wealth with a parable that compares the rich man (symbolic of the Pharisees) and Lazarus, a poor man (symbolic of the kingdom of God). As you read this parable, keep in mind how the rich man treats poor Lazarus while they are both alive upon the earth. Then afterward, when they both die, take note of how the forceful tactics used by the rich man to force and push his way into the kingdom of God are of no avail when he pleads his case.

This is the whole reason Jesus tells the parable after He teaches about the violence that is forcing their way into the kingdom. Poor Lazarus is a truth seeker and the rich man symbolic of the Pharisees is destitute in the sight of God (Luke 16:19-31). Read Luke 16:31 and compare it with Luke 16:16. In Luke 16:16, Jesus says, *"The Law and the Prophets were proclaimed until John* (the Baptist); *since that time the gospel of the kingdom of God has been preached, and everyone is forcing his way into it" (New American Standard Bible).* Jesus IS the fulfillment of ALL the Law and what the Prophets taught, declared, and bore witness to; that is, the Law was given because of disobedience and the Prophets foretold of God's redemption through one of David's descendants who would ascend to the throne of Israel and reign forever in the eternal kingdom of God. Here before these Pharisees stood the Blessed Hope of Israel. But they were blinded and unable to perceive who Jesus was because of their violent manner of life. They were so accustomed to using force and severity to dominate God's children that when the kingdom of God was preached to them, they tried unsuccessfully to use their same old forceful tactics.

These self-righteous Pharisees were the ones who had foremost knowledge of the Law and the Prophets, but, because they were always forcing their way on others by pushing, crowding, and using whatever means necessary to obtain wealth, status, and power, they were blinded and could not hear the gospel of the kingdom of God (see John 1:6-34 *"For the Law was given through Moses; grace and truth were realized through Jesus Christ"* (John 1:17 NAS).

The many greedy workers of darkness that hide behind the word Christian would do well to heed the warnings given here. Greedy and over-controlling leadership is rampant and getting worse! Churches rob the people under the guise of tithes and offerings." The money collected by so-called Christian ministries and churches does very little to help the needy. Much of the tithes and offerings collected either line the pockets of ministers or go into supporting manmade structures and funding the 501C-3 tax-exempt organization. This is simply a fact. A very little percentage of the money given to Christian ministries and churches goes to helping the disadvantaged. I remember being in a fellowship that had a food pantry but it was used to fill the pastor, family, and parishioners' bellies first; the leftovers were given to those who had a need, and sometimes the food would be days to weeks old. Tell me how this is the will of God or even a blessing to those who have a true need. Thank God the needy are like Lazarus and they will be the ones who enter the kingdom of God. But woe to those who have neglected them!

Violent Men Who Take by Force – More Accounts

Throughout the twentieth century and into the twenty-first century, the majority of Christian preachers and teachers have assumed the violent men who take the kingdom by force refers to mighty men of faith who fight the devil victoriously. As I have already explained, the context of Matthew 11:12 is of Jesus addressing the Pharisees, a sect of evil men who attacked the kingdom of God through various means.

All the people revered John the Baptist and held him to be a true prophet of the Most High. The Pharisees' first attempt at forcing their way into the kingdom of God was via John the Baptist's ministry; they did this by seeking to be baptized by him to save face in the eyes of the people. John the Baptist rebuked them, and so they plotted against him. The following narratives of John the Baptist's ministry show how both the Jews and Herod acted as violent me" attempting to take the kingdom by force (see Matthew 3:1-17).

John the Baptist was dressed in rough clothing, proclaiming a simple message of the kingdom... —*"Repent!"* Multitudes came to him, being baptized and confessing their sins. However, when the Pharisees and Sadducees came to John, he refused to baptize them calling them, *"You brood of vipers, who warned you to flee from the wrath to come?"* (Matt. 3:7, Luke 3:7)

John knew they were not in keeping the kingdom of God; they were there solely to further their empire, their legacy, their dominion, their self-existence, and the kingdom of darkness. As in the other gospel accounts, John told them that without true repentance, *"And the ax is already laid at the root of the trees; every tree therefore that does not bear good fruit is cut down and thrown into the fire"* (Matt. 3:10, Luke 3:9). This is in keeping with Jesus's teaching in Luke chapter 16 and the parable of Lazarus and the rich man; the rich man was thrown into the eternal fire as would the Jews.

John the Baptist marked the beginning of the preaching of the kingdom of God. Until then, as Jesus said in Luke chapter 16, only the Law and the Prophets had been spoken; until John's time, only the Law and the future prophecies of Jesus the Messiah had been pronounced. Now that Jesus was alive and in his public ministry, the kingdom of God was being preached widely and openly. Finally, after 4,000 years, mankind would have true redemption, which can only come through Jesus, God's only begotten Son (John 3:16). John affirmed this by becoming, *"The voice of one crying in the wilderness, Make ready the way of the Lord, make His paths straight."* (Isa. 40:3, Mal. 3:1, Matt. 3:3, Mark 1:3; Luke

3:4). John knew that at long last Yahweh was revealing Himself and His character accurately through the life of His only begotten Son, Jesus. John said of Jesus, *"And all flesh shall see the salvation of God"* (Luke 3:6).

Let's examine John 3:23-4.3 scripture more. This passage reaffirms both John the Baptist and Jesus were proclaiming the kingdom of God, and that violent men (i.e., the Pharisees, Scribes, and all who could not see) were trying to force their way into the kingdom of God through cunning and violence. The typical presupposition by teachers and ministers in Christendom does not hold any water here because neither John nor Jesus took the kingdom by force. When Jesus heard the Pharisees were coming, He departed and went to a different region. That cannot be construed as taking the kingdom by force.

John the Baptist concedes that he is not the Christ and that he must decrease so that Jesus's role as Messiah could increase. This is not taking the kingdom by force in any way, shape, or form. John said to those who claimed to be his disciples:

> *A man can receive nothing unless it has been given him from heaven. You yourselves are my witnesses that I said, 'I am not the Christ,' but, 'I have been sent ahead of Him. He who has the bride is the bridegroom; but the friend of the bridegroom, who stands and hears him, rejoices greatly because of the bridegroom's voice. So this joy of mine has been made full. He must increase, but I must decrease. He who comes from above is above all, he who is of the earth is from the earth and speaks of the earth. He who comes from heaven is above all. What He has seen and heard, of that He testifies; and no one receives His testimony. He who has received His testimony has set his seal to this,*

that God is true. For He whom God has sent speaks the words of God; for He gives the Spirit without measure. The Father loves the Son and has given all things into His hand. He who believes in the Son has eternal life; but he who does not obey the Son will not see life, but the wrath of God abides on him. John 3:27-36 KJV.

How did the Jewish leaders as violent men attempt to force their way into the kingdom of God? John answers this question saying of them, *"And no man receives His witness"* (John 3:32). This statement refers primarily to the unbelieving amongst the Jewish religious leaders. We know this is true because later in the context it reads, *"When therefore the Lord knew that the Pharisees had heard that Jesus was making and baptizing more disciples than John* (although Jesus Himself was not baptizing, but His disciples were), *He left Judea, and departed again into Galilee"* (John 4:1, Driver & Kilpatrick 1900, Cambridge Edition).

Ironically, this is similar to what we see happening in Christianity today. Any time a man of God begins to proclaim God's truth, the leadership of the religious machine known as Christianity begins to muscle in on the kingdom of God, often forcing God's true people into obscurity.

Again, I must stress this is not a book that will present psychoanalysis of why things persist but rip the covers off the beast that lurks within our very beings that strikes out at every entity that comes to kill, steal, and destroy the individuals of God.

Chapter 3

Nature of Sin–The Beast and Falling into Ritualism

Follow me as I begin to carry you through a supposition of belief and the deduction of faith. Struggles of self-doubt, insecurity, self-loathing, and lack of confidence stand as *"ever learning, and never able to come to the knowledge of the truth"* (2 Tim. 3:7 KJV), *"seeing but not able to perceive, hearing but not able to understand"* (Mark 4:12 KJV).

I give you another account that took place in my life. I remember waddling in self-deprivation, hoping this tailor-made trial would only pass, hoping for a reprieve of some sort. Thoughts of inadequacy only existing in my own heart and mind yet coming to maturity and reality questioned were this road promised to me and every born-again believer? Am I truly saved? Have I truly been called, chosen by God? To answer these questions for you, I cannot say; however, the principle of living a sanctified life (set aside/separate from the world and yourself unto the Lord) filled with power and authority is attributed to death to self. *"And he said to them all, If any man will come after me, let him deny himself, and take up his cross daily, and follow me"* (Luke 9:23 (KJV).

As I peruse over my life, I notice that the spirit man was growing in leaps and bounds as my physical person cried out because of the intense mortification of my flesh. When it came to praying, I did not find myself desiring the hours of prayers, the meditations, even lying prone upon my face. I remember the hunger, desire, and thirsting for the sincere milk of the Word as well as the meat—oh, how I could taste and see that the Lord is so good—just as Job stated, *"Neither have I gone back from the commandment of his lips; I have esteemed the words of his mouth more than my necessary food"* (Job 23:12 (KJV).

I realize at that time I had walked away from the commandments of His lips, fighting to pray, struggling to study the Word of God, making excuses, walking in deceit, and malice. I was tussling every step to succumb to the perfect and complete will of God through repentance of the heart, mortifying my flesh and causing the lust of the flesh, the lust of the eyes, and the pride of life to bow down to the perfect and complete will of God. Yet within my members another authority lie in wait for the right opportunity to show forth its ugly, subdued head hidden like a volcano ready to erupt at any time. It focused its betrayal in lost and forgotten dreams and failures in past experiences—that **old nature**. I thought this monster was dead, but yet I found it alive, continuing to make war with the inner man who is Christ the Hope of Glory. This nature seemed to never sleep nor slumber, thriving on confusion, lies, and manipulations of the heart. It stretched its dormant tentacles of hate waiting for the right time to leap into the forefront of my mind without thought of right or wrong, ready with all steadfastness to override the position of faith within my spiritual being.

As I saw this creature and its driving force, I knew I had to mortify its nature. I knew I must kill it and destroy the very hatred that it portrays to be; to stop its hostile head of deceit rising to pursue its agenda in a world that dictates living for self as the epitome of all things. Even as I sit here, I fight to concede to the cup of Christ (death to self), taking on His personality, His characteristics, His life of sufferings and obedience, yet my nature constantly stands up for who and what I want; it cries out for justice, for equality, for existence, to be known, accepted and received. As I fight, I am reminded of Christ in the Garden of Gethsemane. Will this cup pass?

Can't you see it is the tormenting of your flesh that cries out for the spotlight, for the glory, for the honor, and acceptance? It is the flesh as it portrays drops of one's being sliding, kicking, and fighting for its existence, for its place, for its voice in society, deeming those things that are right and just to be unjust and unrighteous. This natural part of our being cries out to be heard and seen, to be loved and adored, to be wanted and. This is not to say these social behaviors of need is wrong, however, it is another thing to glorify and give authority to the one part of self that will lead me into destructive. All I can do is cry out, "Savior, rescue me." Do I pretend, do I put on the costume of Christianity and portray my feathers like a peacock seeking its peahen? As I strive, it appears that no matter how one may attempt to bring about a correction to the flesh, it must be remembered that it takes both the physical and spiritual to subdue the appetite of the flesh. In short, these things come by prayer (the spiritual) and fasting (the physical).

> *But Jesus took him by the hand and lifted him up; and he arose. And when he was come into the house, his disciples asked him privately, Why could not we cast him out? And he said to them, This kind can come*

forth by nothing, but by prayer and fasting. Mark 9:27-29 KJV

I've heard the many swelling accolades about fasting (*"Moreover when ye fast, be not as the hypocrites of a sad countenance: for they disfigure their faces, that they may appear unto men to fast"* Matt. 16:16 KJV.), yet it appears that our old nature continues to testify of the much wantonness and cannot help itself. This leads us to believe that no matter how one attempts the physical outward show of correction, the flesh (the fallen nature) will continue to find a way to stick out its foul, perverted, obnoxious head to show its ability to survive and strive regardless of what is going on.

As I pressed forward those moments ago, the shadows of self-doubt and self-loathing, the questions of yesteryears, and thoughts and desires bombarded my soul. I wanted this cup to pass, wanted my flesh to cease its hunger and thirst after the world even in the midst of it gripping my throat and causing me to succumb to its tasty dainties of life's pleasures. I failed

Do you know that resisting blood has not taken a hold of this flesh, however, because through Christ I know I will serve Him and He only will I serve? So, this beast that refuses to die to self in any fashion became a thorn in my spiritual existence. However, I found that if I submitted both physically and spiritually as the Scripture has designed, the correction of my flesh by chastising and resisting this old nature through the rudiments of fasting and prayer continuously ceased he beast's torment of my soul. But as I have heard in my Christian walk, to believe that one's flesh has been crucified one time is only a myth, one that shows forth deception and foolishness as a self-righteousness individual makes God's word a lie, and in understanding Christianity, the

Word of God is our road map to a successful daily life, we worship in spirit and truth.

As I think on this entity which I believed was dead, it remained alive and thriving. Hidden? No, it wasn't. Mortified, but not dead. It resided under an assumed character, operating in strength, vitality, and consistency. I'm not speaking in terms of a drug that alters ego or dampers the voices that come to discuss behavior, schemes, and tactics. No, I speak of the beast that so easily besets me and you, the flesh that was formed and shaped in the very image of God Almighty as He spoke in the garden *"let us make man"* (Gen. 1:26 KJV). Yet this glorious body is corrupted by one man's disobedience and sustained through Christ our mediator into obedience. I have found that the more I suffer in this flesh, the more I see God Almighty moving in my life. Therefore, I rejoice in knowing that *"I can do all things through Christ which strengtheneth me"* (Phil. 4:13 KJV).

However, do I request or speak of suffering and pain, do I dare ask for this calamity to follow me daily? No. I have never requested this continually badgering of my flesh to bring me to my knees only to say yes to God's will. Yet I have come to endure as a good soldier for I have asked God to remove this plague from me thrice and still to this day. I hear, *"My grace is sufficient for thee"* (2 Cor. 12:9). Though I cry out, "How long, oh majestic God, how long will thou forsake and not answer when I call?", I yet still hear the resounding brass play a melodic tune, *"My grace is sufficient for thee,"* so I humbly bow to the successor, to the Lord and Savior of my life, for it is by Him (Jesus) and through Him I have life. Therefore, I write today out of obedience to <u>rip the cover off</u> (reveal) of the world's most notorious killer, deceiver, and protestor – THE FLESH, the worker of Satan. Again, I consider the enemy in the mirror.

Even as many thoughts run through me as I continue to write, I am reminded of several times in this journey that my heart became troubled with what has and what is now happening in the church. I'm not speaking of a building, temple, or hall that holds to a religious sect or denomination, but the rather church of God's people as we see today. The Christ whom I love, obey and live—to doubt who and what He is based on what one has learned while growing from a child is not the Christ who we read about and serve in the Word of God.

This is not about judging those of you who want to justify your lifestyle of self-wants, but to open one's mind to the deception of one's flesh as it continues to perpetuate its worth throughout this world as we know it to be. I will not point the finger and say that many have not taught the true Christ of the Word of God, rather have taken a little of God's word and put a whole lot of their theology, traditions, culture, rudiments, and belief system to transform the true and living God into the demigod of covetousness, hate, greed, and immorality. It is all about self-centered me-ism—look at me, pat me on my back, exalt me, I'm this, I have this title, I have this wealth, I have this degree, I have this prestige, this power, this substance, this is my legacy. These self-righteous and self-indulgent people turn the truth of God into a two-footed beast so that they may be able to touch, see, and worship. These people, who profess to be the all-knowing of God's Word and life, who execute the falsehoods of Christianity under a cloak of hypocritical lifestyle, lay wait to deceive like a lion, ready to devour the sheep of God.

Calling forth a picture of the baby Christ lying in a manger without power and authority of our Lord as a mere prophet who has no authority nor power, that falls to the lust of the flesh, the lust of the eyes, and the pride of life. Just merely saying and thinking that Jesus, this one hundred percent Godman in the flesh given all power by God the Father, is incapable of delivering you from yourself and every given reason, purpose, thought, and deed **is a lie.** It is a lie of complete devastation that has trickled down through the ages of Christianity and continues to move throughout Christianity today as the new Babylonian doctrine of Jesus the Christ, fostering allegiance to Balaam. Sleeping, raping and pissing on the holy things of God Almighty breeds skepticism, disbelief, doubts, and confusion in the minds of newborn babes of God. Religious sects fight amongst themselves for dominance, allowing hate to spread like butter upon freshly baked bread. Denomination against denomination, sect against sect, this teaching against that teaching, this lifestyle against that lifestyle, all are the commandments of men with their laws, precepts, rudiments, and legalities that– choke the very existence, the very knowledge of God the Father from the mind. Many false prophets that reach from the abyss of their doctrines have taken to preaching and coercing you as a disciple of Christ to mimic as they do to inherit the kingdom of God that you now walk upon through the lust of the flesh, the lust of the eyes, and the pride of life. Visions of spirits in one's mind bring forth doctrines of devils. This doctrine has no power, no authority, and has no victory; let me make it plain...no success (2 Corinthians 11:13-15). This is an apostasy (a falling away from the truth) of all doctrine that satan himself has preached and caressed from the time he was cast out of heaven with a third of the angels.

This doctrine continues to tell Christians that if they are not a prosperous tycoon, they are not blessed. It tells them that God doesn't mind them cheating, lying, and indulging in bestiality and other sexual misconduct which causes the desire whore after all ungodliness. It proclaims that if they do not believe what I believe, do what I do, or even wear what I wear, they will not go to heaven. The myths go on; the chains and bars of words and action that have been placed as stumbling blocks for Gods people have quadrupled in time and yet God's people have almost been crushed to a pulp by the spiritual mafia who extracts protection from the body of believers by pretending to be elders, rabbis, pastors, prophets, ministers, missionaries, priest, nuns, evangelists, apostles, deacons/deaconess, and laypeople.

Christians are constantly attacked verbally and even physically slaughtered daily, fearing the rape of their children (hearing their cries of spiritual agony) as they await captivity by the false religious' many words and flamboyant lifestyle. Where is our hope, as I hear so many screams out? It is in Jesus of Nazareth, the true and only Christ, the Anointed One, the Messiah, and our Lord and Savior. Jesus is The Way, The Truth, and The Life. There never has been and never will be any other Christ, Teacher, Lord, Savior, or form of Consciousness whereby our eternal souls may be saved.

Foremost, the Bible prophesied that there has been and will continue to be an ever-increasing number of powerful and alluring false Christs (anti-Christs) as we draw closer to the return of our Lord and Savior, Jesus. As the body of believers anticipates this forthcoming, the scriptures allude to its validity as this: *"For false Christ and false prophets will rise and show great signs and wonders to deceive, if possible, even the elect"* (Matt. 24:24 NKJV). In understanding the advent of deceivers moving and working through the ranks of the religious realm, Christians continuously need to prepare themselves spiritually so that they will not be taken in by the false teachings. 2 Peter 2:1-3 KJV gives great detail on this problem:

> *But there were false prophets also among the people, even as there shall be false teachers among you, who privily shall bring in damnable heresies, even denying the Lord that bought them, and bring upon themselves*

swift destruction. And many shall follow their <u>pernicious ways</u>. And through covetousness shall they with feigned words make merchandise of you: whose judgment now of a long time lingereth note, and their damnation slumbereth not.

- Shall bring in has reference to introduce or bring in secretly or craftily.

- Pernicious ways have reference to sensuality, lascivious doings, dissolute ways, riotousness, immoral, and destructive.

False cults, liberal churches, occult movements, and false doctrines of every sort are proliferating rapidly all over the world, all speaking in the name of "Jesus" or "the Christ" (but never of "our Lord and Savior Jesus Christ"). As in Scripture, *"because of whom the way of truth shall be evil spoken of. And through covetousness shall they with <u>feigned</u> words make merchandise of you: whose judgement now of a long time lingereth not, and their damnation slumbereth not"* (2 Peter 2:2-3 KJV).

- Feigned gives reference to a false appearance to imitate to deceive.

The word heresies here means to choose in the Greek. It carries the connotation that when people decide they will believe in a false doctrine it is by their own free will/choice (see Judges 2). Normally, there is a conflict in their heart with the true word of God (something they do not wish to conform too) so they begin to justify and make excuses when they find their desires to be in opposition to the will of God. This opposition is called disobedience or self-worship. Self-worship opens the individual spiritually to deception because deep down they are seeking a way to avoid coming under the complete authority of God and His Word. Just adhering to bits and pieces of God's Word that fits one's motive of operation entraps a person in physical and spiritual immortality that is not the way of Holiness –

> *"For I am the Lord your God: ye shall therefore sanctify yourselves, and ye shall be holy; for I am holy: neither shall ye defile yourselves with any manner of creeping thing that creepeth upon the earth"* (Lev. 11:44).

> *"Speak unto all the congregation of the children of Israel, and say unto them, Ye shall be holy: for I the Lord your God am holy"* (Lev. 19:2).

> *"Because it is written, Be ye holy; for I am holy"* (1 Peter 1:16).

> (NOTE: Holy – be one in substance with God.)

Whether you acclaim to Christianity or not, are a born again believer or not, or a leader or a follower, Peter tells us that *"And through covetousness "* (2 Peter 2:3 KJV). This phrase contains the Greek word "pleonexia" (Mickelson Strong's Concordance 2015) that means *greediness,* or *the desire to have more.* The spirit of the translation refers to a person wanting more for self who will go through great means to get it. By no means does this word mean it is a sin to desire more; there are many instances in which this desire can be honorable, such as desiring more knowledge and wisdom of God and His Word. However, *pleonexia* postulates it is an unholy ambition that desires to not only have what other people own and exploit them both in the lustful sense and the sense of control. To see this action working in line with the word of God, you might think of the perverted, ambitious leaders who have used the Word of God to sexually abuse women, men, boys, and girls. Another example is how these faulty leaders steal and rape the people of God to get their mansions, cars, furs, titles, power, authority, and legacy. The man or woman who has this ambition essentially desires to usurp the place of Christ in people's lives and create themselves to be demigods causing believers to take their eyes off of the true Christ and begin to serve the creature more than the Creator (see Paul speaking in Rom. 1:16-20 KJV).

More so, Peter announces this mode of deception as false teaching and deceptive words. The effect of false teaching is blatant immorality. The Greek word "aselgeia" describes the attitude of people who have lost their shame and have lost the fear of God. It is used in Jude 1:4 as lewdness where we read about ungodly men: *"For there are certain men crept in unawares, who were before of old ordained to this condemnation, ungodly men, turning the grace of our God into lasciviousness, and denying the only Lord God, and our Lord Jesus Christ."* Take for example the first lady of a ministry I came across who sexually raping young, abused women she had befriended, expressing that this is the will of God and God Almighty accepts this behavior. How about a Prophet prophesying to young women and men that it is alright to do sexual favors for him/her because it will allow them to get closer to God and would cause them to be highly favored? The list of lasciviousness in the church goes on.

In true form, we must be very careful to compare everything we see and hear with God's Word and not believe everything that is proclaimed by men. God will not allow us to live on the advice of others. Rather, He intends that we learn to seek guidance from the Holy Spirit which is accomplished only when we diligently seek Him and wait on Him. *("In all thy ways acknowledge him, and he shall direct thy paths"* Prov. 3:6 KJV). God promises that He is a rewarder of those who diligently seek Him as it says in Hebrews 11:6 KJV: *"But without faith it is impossible to please him: for he that cometh to God must believe that he is, and that he is a rewarder of them that diligently seek him."* God will not let us down if we wait patiently for Him.

However, the doctrine of self-worship continues to tell the individual that they are bound by the actions, devices, and pressures of Satan and his workers of darkness. This doctrine is the voice of the anti-Christ who has walked from the backstreets of hell as a novice to be arrayed in fine linens of the pulpits of our hearts.

Walk with me on this journey against self-centeredness, self-conceitedness, self-esteem, self-glorying, and self. Life, in general, brings about things, situations, and circumstances that will perplex us. When faced with this, some individuals seek psychologists to probe their minds to see if they can solve the problems while others seek out psychologists in hopes that a drug prescribed will remove the haunting and the uncontrollable urges that society states are ethical, acceptable, or part of the normal humanistic response. Still more seek counseling from psychics the occult, and the false allusion of New Age movements to soothe the pain of dark bewilder pasts, hoping that the overpowering urges of failure, shame, and calamity will go away. Yet this route to the dark side of our psyche is not enough to quench the monster within us that urges for roaring evil. Finally, to no avail, after we tried everything else, we begin to seek people (false-teachers and pastors), places, and things that represent or look like the meaning of God to stop the tormenting. When all this doesn't work, people become agnostics or atheists. They try to ignore, pacify, and subdue the demons that thrust out its attitudes, its allegiance, and its belief in a world of self-worship and self-righteous living. Now what was deemed good has become evil and that which is evil has now become good.

This war is consistent with the destruction of the spiritual man. What has taken place is the enemy's campaign of perpetual warfare against the inner man to bring it into the captivity of lust and sin that leads to destruction. Such warfare works mischief in one's mind, moving you closer and closer to imprisonment until finally you will not think about or desire God in your life. This is the enemy's professional job with you. He wants you to believe you are in control and have it all together with none of it resulting from God. However, the Scripture states, *"Behold, all souls are mine: as the soul of the father, so also the soul of the son is mine: the soul that sinneth (continue to sin), it shall die"* (Ezek. 18:4).

Here we wrestle once again with the beast that is within us that drives us to refuse to comply, to obey the will of God. Hearing the voice of the Lord, and yet still refusing to turn to God Almighty who calms the storms in our self-exalted life of lust of the eyes, the lust of the flesh and pride of life. It is something to still believe that we are in control or having it all together when all hell is exploding in our lives. We hide behind disguises of falsehood, positions, and titles thinking that this will someway open the door to heaven without living, walking, and worshiping the true and living God. Why is it so easy to give so much allegiance to person, place, or things? To lie, cheat, and manipulate to receive the accolades from those who do not have our best wishes. Is money so important – is it not a tool? Are fame and fortune, so needed that you would sell your child for a fix of popularity and recognition. These are thoughts of selfish desires for no one but yourself.

Cares of Life

Time and time again, people fall trapped in its sweet, yet bitter and dysfunctional way of life. The flesh wraps itself in a method of triviality: "the cares of this life". A disillusioned doctrine that the flesh succumbs to, killing, stealing, and destroying the very essence of whom and what Christ accomplished on Golgotha road.

The Scriptures tell us not to get caught up in the cares of life (Luke 21:34) for if we are obedient to God, He will take care of all our needs (Phil. 4:19). So then why do we not believe that God can? I have found that people say they believe and do the opposite; in concept, they do not believe. However, I have concluded that God has a way of bringing you back to yourself. He can break every fetter in your life, placing you on the straight and narrow road which leads (and continues to lead) you to the everlasting life. Even as you look at the fork which separates you from life and death, God ensures that if you belong to Him, you will move toward Him, toward Life.

I'm not speaking of forcing and manipulating; I speak of coming to the authority of submission to the Lord and Savior of your life—<u>just agreeing with God</u>. Wanting to be delivered, wanting to be saved, not just looking for a temporary fix but receiving a permanent solution to one's dysfunctional, inapt life (*"And ye shall know the truth, and the truth shall make you free"* John 8:32.). Once the storm is over and the wind begins to calm as it brushes the cheeks of the believer —this is the peace that surpasses all understanding (Phil. 4:7) and brings one to the conclusion that Jesus is the answer. It has taken some a day to grasp and others up to twenty years or more to learn to completely and emphatically trust God without any doubts for He truly cares for us. Emphasizing how long is not the point, but it is a truth that believers will learn as they continue to give of themselves and step towards Jesus who is the VICTORY of all.

This book is not here to beat or destroy hope within you, nor glorify sin or the devices that the enemy uses to achieve the ultimate satisfaction of destroying the very temple of God (you) with the lust of the flesh, the lust of the eyes and the pride of life. Instead, this book is meant to open your spiritual eyes to the devices that are used in our lives and to break the fetter of deception that lies in the action of our flesh. We understand the lust of the flesh for we deal with it daily in all facets of our media. This also plays hand-in-hand with the lust of the eyes. I'm not only speaking of sexual innuendos but covetous natures (wanting more for self or strongly desiring of another, being willing to go to great means to accomplish the task). This is the beast that destroys ministry after ministry, family after family, business after business. It perpetuates a social and unethical behavior that penetrates the very heart and mind of its constituents. It is not concerning of who you may think you are, who you portray to be, or what position you partake in, Its thought and action are to destroy the very God that rests within you.

Let's look at it from another perspective. For example, was it not Dr. King who said that the 11:00 a.m. church hour was the most segregated in America? Unfortunately, not much has improved racially in this country since his time. We as a nation are further divided and fractured along the lines of class, culture, ethnicity, religion, and wealth more so than at any other time in our history. It seems the dividing line between those who have much and those who don't have widened to the point that one out of every three Americans is considered the working poor. Greed, vanity, and obsessive possession of physical wealth have driven this country into a moral abyss of injustice. The fine lines between good and wrong have been blurred. To show compassion, love, and kindness for the widows, fatherless, and orphans are looked upon with suspect and contempt. *"The wicked in his pride doth persecute the poor: let them be taken in the devices that they have imagined"* (Ps. 10:2 KJV).

Those who show empathy toward the terrible predicament of their fellow man are viewed as weak and not of strong moral character. How did things get so twisted in this country where good is considered evil and evil is considered good? It is because we as a nation decided to pursue worldly vanities and not the kingdom of God.

What are the consequences of lusting after power, prestige, and wealth while at the same time having contempt for both your fellow man and God Almighty? As we continue to move towards a lifestyle of the rich and famous, allow me to introduce this thought. In the King James Version Bible, Psalms 49:6-20 reads"

> *They that trust in their wealth, and boast themselves in the multitude of their riches; None of them can by any means redeem his brother, nor give to God a ransom for him: For the redemption of their soul is precious, and it ceaseth for ever: That he should still live for ever, and not see corruption. For he seeth that wise men die, likewise the fool and the brutish person perish, and leave their wealth to others. Their inward thought is, that their houses shall continue for ever, and their dwelling places to all generations; they call their lands after their own names. Nevertheless man being in honour abideth not: he is like the beasts that perish. This their way is their folly: yet their posterity approve their sayings. Selah. Like sheep they are laid in the grave; death shall feed on them; and the upright shall have dominion over them in the morning; and*

their beauty shall consume in the grave from their dwelling. But God will redeem my soul from the power of the grave: for he shall receive me. Selah. Be not thou afraid when one is made rich, when the glory of his house is increased; For when he dieth he shall carry nothing away: his glory shall not descend after him. Though while he lived he blessed his soul: and men will praise thee, when thou doest well to thyself. He shall go to the generation of his fathers; they shall never see light. Man that is in honour, and understandeth not, is like the beasts that perish.

Just as the rich man suffered eternal damnation in hell while the angels cuddled Lazarus, so too should be the plight of those who choose to pursue a path of vanity at the expense of their fellow brethren, whether they acclaim to the Wall Street, corporate America, politics, labor unions, or even the church itself. It does not mean that God does not want you to be successful or be comfortable in your livelihood. He wants you to put Him first in everything that you do. *"Every man also to whom God hath given riches and wealth, and hath given him power to eat thereof, and to take his portion, and to rejoice in his labour; this is the gift of God"* (Eccl. 5:19). God wants, expects, and commands us to look after the widowed, the orphans, and the fatherless. *"Thus speaketh the LORD of hosts, saying, Execute true judgment, and shew mercy and compassions every man to his brother: And oppress not the widow, nor the fatherless, the stranger, nor the poor; and let none of you imagine evil against his brother in your heart"* (Zech. 7:9-10).

However, society has cast aside the poor as a hindrance, a nuisance, and plight. We give more honor, respect, and acknowledgment to the robber barons who come to our houses and churches just because they glitter with gold –

> *My brethren have not the faith of our Lord Jesus Christ, the Lord of glory, with respect of persons. For if there come unto your assembly a man with a gold ring, in goodly apparel, and there come in also a poor man in vile raiment; And ye have respect to him that weareth the gay clothing, and say unto him, Sit thou here in a good place; and say to the poor, Stand thou there, or sit here under my footstool: Are ye not then partial in yourselves, and are become judges of evil thoughts? Hearken, my beloved brethren, Hath not God chosen the poor of this world rich in faith, and heirs of the kingdom which he hath promised to them that love him? But ye have despised the poor. Do not rich men oppress you, and draw you before the judgment seats? Do not they blaspheme that worthy name by the which ye are called? If ye fulfil the royal law according to the scripture, Thou shalt love thy neighbour as thyself, ye do well: But if ye have respect to persons, ye commit sin, and are convinced of the law as transgressors. For whosoever shall keep the whole law, and yet offend in one point, he is guilty of all. James 2:1-10*

How do you engage and interact with the less fortunate among you? There are those of us who are less than a stone's throw away from falling into absolute poverty but yet we become hypocritical to those in need. We swallow the bankrupt philosophy of various politicians who describe the plight of the twenty-five million unemployed in this country as their fault while at the same celebrating the excessiveness of the extremely wealthy and those who steal from the public coffers to prop up their failing financial empires. America, wake up for the judgment of God is at hand. Will you surrender to God or will you continue seeking worldly possession? Will you worship at the synagogue of Satan? *"Behold, I will make them of the synagogue of Satan, which say they are Jews, and are not, but do lie; behold, I will make them come and worship before thy feet, and to know that I have loved thee"* (Rev. 3:9).

In our churches, we teach a false message of prosperity based on the ill pursuit of economic riches instead of seeking the kingdom of God. Malcolm X stated fully, "We do not condemn the preachers as an individual, but we condemn what they teach. We urge that the preachers teach the truth, to teach our people the one important guiding rule of conduct-unity of purpose" (Malcolm X Quotes 2020). Christ was correct when He called the activities that went on in the house of worship during the era *"a den of thieves"*:

> *"And Jesus went into the temple of God, and cast out all them that sold and bought in the temple, and overthrew the tables of the moneychangers, and the seats of them that sold doves, And said unto them, It is written, My house shall be called the house of prayer; but ye have made it a den of thieves"* (Matt. 21:12-13).

It is living by and obeying the word of God and not the reckless pursuit of wealth that will give you eternal damnation.

> *"For the love of money is the root of all evil: which while some coveted after, they have erred from the faith, and pierced themselves through with many sorrows"* (1Tim. 6:10).

The coming of God is like a thief in the night. No amount of wealth will save you from the throne of judgment. No position, power, or influence will stay the hand of God when He punishes you for your transgressions. The filthy quest for lucre has and continues to blind many from the sanctuary and protection of God Almighty. *"Feed the flock of God which is among you, taking the oversight thereof, not by constraint, but willingly; not for filthy lucre, but of a ready mind"* (1 Pet. 5:2). The lust of money, power, and the absence of love for one's neighbor, friend, or even enemy have transformed people into ravenous wolves. Hatred of your brother for money sake constitutes murder. *"Whosoever hateth his brother is a murderer: and ye know that no murderer hath eternal life abiding in him"* (1 John 3:15).

If you have plenty due to the sweat of your brow through hard work, honesty, and humility, then God is pleased. After all, you have honored Him because you acknowledge that He has made the way possible. God commands us to pursue a worthy vocation to provide for the needs of our families. He expects those who are not in need but prefer to sponge off the labors of others to seek a livelihood. *"The words of a talebearer are as wounds, and they go down into the innermost parts of the belly"* (Prov. 18:8). Perpetuating a lie to get over on your fellow brethren to steal their hard-earned wages and livelihood is a blasphemy against God.

> *"But now ye also put off all these; anger, wrath, malice, blasphemy, filthy communication out of your mouth"* (Col 3:8),

> *"And in the same house remain, eating and drinking such things as they give: for the labourer is worthy of his hire"* (Luke 10:7 KJV).

> *"For the scripture saith, thou shalt not muzzle the ox that treadeth out the corn. And, The labourer is worthy of his reward"* (1 Tim. 5:18 KJV).

This refers to the fact that care must be considered toward ministers and those who are laborious in the Gospel. Are not God's sons and daughters worthy of double honor and esteem? Is it there just due just as much as the reward of the labourer? These questions are something to think of, however, the apostle Timothy solemnly charges us to guard against partiality. We always have a great need to watch that we do not take advantage of other's hard labor. Remember, in all things we must keep ourselves pure in thoughts and deed, not raping and robbing the people of God for personal gain. Timothy also charges us to take care of our and our brother's health. We are not to make our bodies masters, though neither slaves, but to use them so that they may be most helpful to us in the service of God.

Do you know there are secrets sins and there are open sins? God will bring to light the hidden things of darkness and make known the counsels of all hearts. Looking forward to the judgment day, let us all attend to our proper offices, whether in higher or lower stations, watching that the name and doctrine of God may never be blasphemed on our account.

These are uncertain times that we live in. As Christians, we must step forward to stand for justice. Let our voices be heard for the oppressed, and let us not verbally say words but becoming an advocate for the poor and socially indifferent. Our words of empathy must become action-oriented and not meaningless rhetoric. Every day, many of our fellow countrymen continue to face the foreclosure of their homes, losing their jobs, having their vehicles repossessed, losing family and friends to drugs, sex slavery and so much more. We cannot stand idly by and do nothing because one of our friends, family members, saints in the church, or co-workers could be next. We must gather our resources, contacts, and networks to help find jobs, homes, and sources of transportation for people to get back and forth for work, counseling, rehabs, etc. Church-going folks should be behind faith-based initiatives that expose the corruption of power, such as the draconian voting laws that have been passed in dozens of states to disenfranchise millions of Black and Latino voters. If we remain silent, then the perpetrators of injustice against the poor, disadvantaged, and widows will continue to pursue an aggressive agenda to hollow out this nation financially until hardly anyone will have the means to earn a decent living. The only true wealth is in knowing that God will provide us with the necessities of life and that we cannot do it by ourselves. Prosperity ministries and the pursuit of wealth at any cost are contrary to the will of God; they pull all who dare to go down such a path in the wilderness of the world. Therefore, I ask you today how long will you live for the beast?

Chapter 4

Deception

Fear had set in my soul as hot buttered popcorn in the shallow seats of a movie theatre. I've always felt that nothing could separate me from the love of God until, one day, I was faced with my greatest fear. It wasn't the pain of not feeling wanted, not being accepted or loved, nor was it my financial instability, but the seduction of the mind—deception.

We understand that God, as children created by the Most High, we are fearfully and wonderfully made: *"I will praise thee; for I am fearfully and wonderfully made: marvelous are thy works; and that my soul knoweth right well"* (Ps. 139:14). And those things that God has placed in us to be a natural affection to the opposite sex is both good and acceptable when it is in its proper place. However, when you allow impure thoughts, desires, and wants to come within your temple and begin to entertain and lay with them, here arranged in all of its settings and glory begins sin (the lust of the flesh). Therefore, we must confess these demons of doubt, disbelief, fear, loneliness, despair, despondency, and pride as the cloaking device of our imperfection. These demons latch themselves onto an individual, and that's when you find yourself falling deeper and deeper into its sinful clutches. You are not in total submission to the Holy Spirit and Truth. People find themselves seeking answers when the answer has already expressed, felt, and understood. *"Having eyes, see ye not? And having ears, hear ye not? And do ye not remember?"* (Mark 8:18).

If this fault of lust is revealed in you, it will cause great destruction to you, your family, and those in fellowship with you if you indulge in its fantasy and misguided realities. It isn't the outward sin that others may see, however, *"Take us the foxes, the little foxes, that spoil the vines: for our vines have tender grapes"* (Song of Sol. 2:15). These are hidden sins that only the Holy Ghost can see and discern.

Let's park here for a moment and discuss the small foxes and what is meant by this scripture. If we, God's people, would enjoy his presence and blessing, we must put away every iniquity (injustice or immorality; immoral act) and obstacle (something that stands in the way of achieving a goal or of understanding something) that separates us from the life purpose of serving and worshiping God. Once we become converted, we must contend for the faith, watching for the subtlety of the enemy's devices at all times. *"Search me, O God, and know my heart: try me, and know my thoughts: And see if there be any wicked way in me and lead me in the way everlasting"* (Ps. 139:23-24).

Little foxes spoil the vines, and little sins do mischief to the tender heart. Even within a group of spiritual people, you will find pressure. I'm talking about peer pressure. These pressures begin to bombard your soul, mind, and body like a cyclone hitting the side of a building and carrying it away to nothingness. Looking for liberty in Christ within believers, you become enslaved to the rudiments of the world and traditions of men (*"Beware lest any man spoil you through philosophy and vain deceit, after the tradition of men, after the rudiments of the world, and not after Christ"*(Col. 2:8 KJV), no longer seeking the Lord but compromising the standards of Christ just to have others accept you. It is open season for destruction. You become open bait for all to partake of and for the enemy to come upon you; running never escaping, seeking yet not finding, and knocking yet hoping for the door to open, finally calling out of desperation until you have no more energy to cry out. From the depths of your soul you beg, "Who can save me from this body of sin? Who can rescue me from this body of death? Why must I die? Why can I not yet hold onto me?"

Let's look from a standpoint of victory as I express my triumph in hopes it will help you when your emotions and desires seem to overtake you. I remember a time in my life before I was married where I felt I had to compromise in the church (body of believers) to keep the remarks, attitudes, malice, and hatred from its continual plaguing moves upon my soul. The flesh, whether in the form of loneliness, wantonness, or any other mode of operation, will have you agreeing to anything just to feel wanted, needed, liked, and or accepted.

Personal Account – Brief Testimony

On a certain day, my blood rushed through my veins as if someone had set me on fire. I recognized this beast (my flesh). The plague of loneliness was more prevalent than ever before in my life. Flesh lusting for flesh. I closed my eyes as if I want, my desire would cease. Then slowly, like a movie being played in front of me, I opened my eyes as the wind gently blew through my hair. Did I see a man in the distance—was it real or a mirage? – As I tried to wipe my eyes in doubt for the first time in more than five years, I felt something happening within my members—the yearning for a man.

As I continued to look through a sunny, hot, and boisterous day, he slowly walked up to me. I began to exhale, and he said to me "I want to be a father to your children and a man to your bed." In astonishment and shock, I wondered how this man could somehow hear my thoughts or did he just read my body language? Was I so transparent that I was an open book a single woman needing a man to justify her, to complete her, and even make her whole? Yet with every morsel of truth within me, I stepped back as if he softly whispered my name, yet saying nothing, I turn from him and walked into the church. I had been approached many times, but this was somewhat different, for I had based part of my ministry on the fact of abstinence – and how I had overcome the many temptations upon me, the moral and physical sins such as drugs, cheating, lying, drinking, and stealing.). But this moment was not like anything I had ever understood or experienced. I stood questioning my intentions, questioning my walk with God, and questioning my seven years of being kept by God since I said yes to Him.

I did not seek this man out; he sought me. I was vulnerable, looking for new fellowship. I felt the pressure due to seeing him in and out of service. He was taunting me with his politeness, his smoothness, and his flirtatiousness. Sweet whispers of melancholy spoken so ever softly yet firm within me. He spoke and I listened; he talked and I dreamed and yearned for his touch. What is happening to me? Since my last relationship, which was my first marriage, I was trapped to a fantasy of what a relationship (marriage) should be; it did not include brokenness, lies, being emotionally abused, talked down too, stripped of any dignity, only to be finally left for emotional and spiritual apostasy where self-hatred became the principal thought.

I had lost all feelings and understanding of what marriage is and what it could. I had turned away from thinking of having and being with someone to be the living and being that God wanted me to be. My marriage had left me shattered and I was warding off men due to being badly hurt. Therefore, there was no thought of companionship since I had said yes to God's will (rededication). I had promised myself I would not fall into lust trap as before with Satan himself. I would not be drawn away by my lust and entice.

Yet I found something that appeared to be stronger than God's will at that moment. It was <u>my flesh</u>—its desires, its wants, and needs. Deception had played me like a deck of phony cards. I did not have to ask someone to deceive me for I had deceived myself. I could hear and feel my pulse rapidly increasing as I watched this man across the room. I could not understand this as it was never spoken of in the Bible classes, women's meetings, seminars, or retreats. I had been evangelizing for close to ten years at this point and I had not felt this emotion before, not even when I was married. What was it?

As I sat and fought, I pondered each thought, and, finally, as clear as day, I heard as if someone was standing right beside me, "It is your FLESH." I realized I had been acting as if I could not feel the passions of the flesh, that thing that was hidden from the world, and yet present with me;– I carried it, I pampered it, and called it a "piece of me". Satan himself brought me my kryptonite; – it was wrapped in voluminous, fine garments, arrayed in the exceptional protocol, and conversed in scholarly verbiage. I was fooled almost, persuaded almost, but not yet.

After hearing the word flesh spoken within me, I was convicted, startled. But it wasn't enough for as soon as I opened my eyes and saw him across the room, I began to focus on the way his body moved; I captured and held tight to every gesture, every facial expression as if they would have escaped. I closed my eyes, feeling his breath against my skin melting the insecurities away, saying with each breaking syllable, "All is well, all is well my love." Finally, I released every thought of pleasure, falling into his arms as a deer lapping water from a brook, focusing on his deep brown eyes as one looking into a canvass of sweet memories. I waited on each savory moment as his body caressed the space of my thoughts.

I asked how could I escape this heartfelt journey that only I knew existed? I heard words that only amounted to nothingness—a little piece of a man is better than none. Lost without feelings, helpless to the flesh's desires and wants, I fought within myself, binding every desire that would have me trapped like heifers in a pin of bulls waiting to be pounded upon in lust. I escaped. In exhaustion, I grabbed hold of my emotions and shook myself back to reality. Repent. I understood exactly what Paul was speaking of, the weight of my flesh was weighing me down, the desire of wanting to be wanted even as the loneliness propagated its persuasion, pulling me into the depths. I cried out, "Lord, help me deliver me, rescue your child." Just as Joseph left his garment in the hands of Potiphar's wife's, I escape with my integrity and faith intact.

Deceived and Being Deceived by One's Desires.

The flesh will have you yearning, desiring, and wanting a man no different than what you've had before. Oh, how the enemy will walk with your flesh, allowing you to feel, taste, and desire the things that will kill, steal, and destroy your existence, your career, your health, and your family. I pause here for a moment and ask why do we always become attracted to the same ole thing? Why is it so easy to step back into relationships, things, places, or situations like those we've experienced before? As I ponder on these thoughts, as I have many times, I've come to understand it is because I am familiar with the perception, deception, and ease of feeling when it comes to these things, persons, or situations. For example, if I was a woman who continuously found Mr. Right as an abuser of the flesh, body, and spirit, or one who is selfish, egotistical, and womanizer, I would constantly find myself attracted to this same type of man no matter how many times I've escaped.

In many situations, whether male or female, we continue to run to this destruction of self-hatred or self-doubt, searching for acceptance and the feeling (not thought) of wanting to be wanted and even controlled. This mindset will allow you to fall back into the warped, broken, dysfunctional relationships that previously held you bound. In reality, we must confess that we know that the bells or whatever else rings are signaling "Please step away from this man/woman and/or situation," and yet we know our flesh will run after it like a lion after a gazelle. Our desires want, and self-defeated attitude will even verbally or psychologically justify what it wants due to the familiarity of old dysfunctional relationships, behaviors, and disrespect with the thought of broken dreams and low self-esteem that wears the costume of inadequacy as though one can have nothing else but misery and pain.

Once the destruction begins its haughty attack, we lie to ourselves move like a locomotive that has been derailed by a pebble laying on the tracks of selfless desires. Finally, with no form of resistance, we submit, knowing good and well if what we know to be true, why could we not make the first, second, or third relationship or situation work. That's right, the flesh will have you "Trippin" on junk, like a fish out of a brook waiting for the next rain. No matter how much you yearn, crave, lust, and affix your daydreams, you'll to succumb false responses and fall into an abyss of hopelessness stripping you, tearing you, and even dragging you from the true foundation of Love which is Jesus, the Rock of Salvation.

Therefore, I ask, why are we expecting different reactions and emotions when we know that the outcome will be the same: *"Ever learning, and never able to come to the knowledge of the truth"*

(2 Tim. 3:7 KJV)? If people do not change their focus and begin to see the picture for what it, they will yearn, chase, and want, potentially finding themselves in another abusive relationship or situation and continuing the cycle of self-hate and low self-esteem to become bitter and withdrawn, full of unforgiveness. We as God's children must change our attitude from a victim to a victor, allowing God Almighty to change the path the continual cycle of self-hatred, letting Him place the balm on our wounds so that our attitudes become healed (whole) and our focus will be on what God has in store for us. We will no longer continually be looking for our gems in all the wrong places

The reason why this is so familiar to you is that the God-given sustaining power has been dragged, stripped, and beaten down in you to a small flicker. It is then you ask, "What is wrong with me? Why do I still yearn for things I know are not beneficial for me, wanting what is not good for me to tell me what I already know?" You see, I understand for I was there. However, the answer is right before you and that is CRY OUT to God. Be real with Him, speak what is in your heart as I did on that day: "Father hold me for I am so weak and need your strength." As I expressed this prayer all kinds of thoughts bombarded my feelings, my emotions ran as a winebibber on payday trying to get that first drink of 'bulldog'. Or going to a club just to walk out with a one night stand or maybe for you it is just trying to get that 1st high again or maybe to be loved, accepted, or even desire – it doesn't matter what the 'beast' maybe but how to get free from the flesh and its' vice-grip is the step that is needed.

The flesh will run crazy. I remember my taste buds yearning for the touch of a man, the caressing of his warm embrace, his firm but coarse skin against my cheek. I wanted the warm embrace of a loving man to his woman and a loving woman to her man as God intended for a husband and wife. Again, I cried out and said,

"Father, help me in my unbelief." As I completed this prayer, I grasped hold of my emotions and found that what I thought was dormant was yet alive, therefore I found that I must practice "mortifying the flesh". *"For if ye live after the flesh, ye shall die: but if ye through the Spirit do **mortify** (to subdue; to abase; to humble; to reduce; to restrain; as inordinate passions, Biblestudytools.com 2020) the deeds of the body, ye shall live"* (Rom. 8:13). So, on that day I did subdue, abase, and restrain myself from the same lifestyle my Heavenly Father had rescued me from. Yielding unto God Almighty's hand is truly the answer.

> *"Mortify therefore your members which are upon the earth; fornication, uncleanness, inordinate affection, evil concupiscence, and covetousness, which is idolatry"* (Col. 3:5).

Practicing temperance (moderation; particularly, habitual moderation regarding the indulgence of the natural appetites and passions) along with mortifying overthrows the lust of the flesh.

> *"But I keep under my body, and bring it into subjection: lest that by any means, when I have preached to others, I myself should be a castaway"* (1 Cor. 9:27).

However, I waited upon God for several more years before I knew and understood I was being kept for the man God prepared me, this day now being married for over fifteen years to a man after God's own heart. I am continuing to fast, continuing to seek God, and continuing all that is required of me. If this can happen to me, I know without a shadow of a doubt that it can happen for you. Just fast and mortify your inordinate passions and watch what God will do in all things.

What Next?

Maybe loneliness, the lust of the eyes and flesh, and even deception is not your demon, but allow me to move into another spirit of the beast as it wraps itself in an array of madness. Perhaps, even as years, months, and days have gone by, you feel as if you still have not truly escaped. You have not been able to define what the madness, the oppression, that is trying to force its beliefs, understanding, greed, and self-pleasure on you. But you will find that as you resist and fight even the harder if you continue mortifying the flesh, you will not fail.

Have you ever thought that holding on has become a way of life for your mere existence? Do you find yourself moving in leaps and bounds from one situation to another, from one circumstance to another, from one earth-shaking existence to the next to no avail? Even though you strive to do and say what is right, it seems you cannot function in a complete state of mind. At the moment you think "peace'" and then chaos breaks out and you are back in a pit, even thinking about the abyss. You see down the path from where you were just months or years ago, friends, family members, and even your foes succeeding while it seems each step you take sinks you deeper and deeper in the quicksand of no return.

Finally, you wonder, "Why can't I get a breakthrough from this turmoil, this chaos?" Then as you go to lick your wounds and feel sorry for yourself, in enters depression wrapped in its garment of self-hate, demonizing you to self-destruction. Desperate and irredeemable, you struggle to get loose from the demons that drive you to this hell-hole of self-destruction through despite everything that is within you, you know you must fight the negativity that has wrapped itself as a bride adornment. Yet you are so tired of the disappointments, the heartaches, and pains, you just want to pull the sheets over your head and just sleep your life away. Hiding as a mole from its predator, you turn within to seclude yourself from those who would strengthen, encourage, and motivate you to live on, hearing from a distance as the raindrops trickle down the hills of Golgotha, a small, still voice ever so gently to you, **"just hold on."**

Another Perception – The Human Heart

Well, my brothers and sisters, that small still voice will not allow you to sink into the muck and the mire; it will constantly fight for your soul, your new life, your existence. That inner man that I speak of is not your subconscious nor conscious mind. It is Christ Jesus, the Hope of Glory, that wraps Himself in the implementation of the Holy Ghost.

His is the small still voice inside telling you, "You can do it, just stay focused. Keep pressing forward, keep enduring and you will overcome." Sometimes it is like having an eternal coach inside of you pushing you unto excellence, the excellence that is in Christ. And then at other times, it may feel as if you are on a major workout to shed those pounds of sin where we say "no pain, no gain". Brothers and sisters, allow me to bring it home for a better and more personal understanding. It is God dragging you unto His perfect and complete will in Him. Our flesh doesn't want to live for Him nor does it want to be obedient to the will of God. Scripture states:

> *Watch and pray, that ye enter not into temptation: the spirit indeed is willing, but the flesh is weak* (Matt. 26:41 KJV).

> *For what the law* (moral law – ten commandments) *could not do, in that it was weak through the flesh, God sending his own Son in the likeness of sinful flesh, and for sin, condemned sin in the flesh: That the righteousness of the law might be fulfilled in us, who walk not after the flesh, but after the Spirit. For they that are after the flesh do mind the things of the flesh; but they that are after the Spirit the things of the Spirit. For to be carnally minded is death; but to be spiritually minded is life and peace. Because the carnal mind is enmity against God: for it is not subject to the law of God, neither indeed can be. So then they that are in the flesh cannot please God. But ye are not in the flesh, but in the Spirit, if so be that the Spirit of God dwell in you. Now if any man have not the Spirit of Christ, he is none of his.* Romans 8:3-9 KJV

The enmity against God, the seed of rebellion and wickedness, the arch-enemy and arch-adversary of all that God stands for, the counsels of the damned, the fallen angels are found in the human heart and the human soul and the human life. We must surrender to the All-Knowing God. He made the first man, perfect and complete in all of his ways, devout and holy and reverent in all of his attitudes, God's perfect workmanship, and yet the enemy of God. The destruction you see before you—our world destroyed, our house (temple of God) burned down in lust, our humanity wrecked with chaos—this is enmity against God which is in us.

> *"And God saw that the wickedness of man was great in the earth, and that every imagination of the thoughts of his heart was only evil continually"* (Gen. 6:5 KJV).

The carnal mind, the mind of the natural man, is enmity itself against God. The mind of the natural man is blackness and rebellion itself it is wickedness itself, it is envy itself. The very essence of sin is found in the human heart.

> *"Because the carnal mind is enmity against God: for it is not subject to the law of God, neither indeed can be"* (Rom. 8:7 KJV).

> *"The mind governed by the flesh is hostile to God; it does not submit to God's law, nor can it do so"* (Rom. 8:7 NIV).

This whole foundation of the man God made has fallen. He has fallen in his mind for his mind is hatred and wrath. He is fallen in his soul for his soul is bound and will be destroyed. He has fallen in his life for his life is filled with the transgression of pride of life, and he has fallen in his desire for his desire is covetousness due to his lust of the flesh and the lust of his eyes. If a man stood before the court of law, the sentence would be death by lethal injection. Romans 8:6 states: *"To be carnally minded is death."* (Romans 8:6a KJV) In Ezekiel 18:20a, the prophet said, *"The soul that sinneth, it shall die."* However, Genesis states: *"But of the tree of the knowledge of good and evil, thou shalt not eat of it: for in the day that thou eatest thereof thou shalt surely die"* (Gen. 2:18 KJV).

The natural carnal mind of man is the enemy of God and the sentence that God has laid upon man is death—universal, everlasting, eternal death. *"And they will go out and look on the dead bodies of those who rebelled against me; the worms that eat them will not die, the fire that burns them will not be quenched, and they will be loathsome to all mankind"* (Isa. 66:24 NIV). That is the fate of the natural, unregenerate man; the sinful nature that is *"the worm that never dies"* (Mark 9:44 KJV). Our corrupt affections must be restrained and mortified by the Holy Spirit.

However, there are many theologians, preachers, philosophers, and scholars as well as learned and powerful me who may know the Christian faith in and out who could conclude, with scientific perception, and say that all men are born good, that the soul is born pure, that life is conceived wholly, and a man is a sinner only because he imitates a sinner. What about the argument about a child will be good if you teach that child's goodness? Or, he or she is to be a sinner they are being taught to be sinful because, by nature, we are pure, holy, and uncorrupt. Moreover, looking from the perspective of the Pauline Theology which gives credence that we are born fallen and corrupt and in sin and that the carnal mind, that is, the natural mind, the mind that we are bought into this world with, is the enemy of God.

Let's look at this closely. King David comments about the degenerated man; that we come into this world with a disposition, a soul, a mind, and a body that are already corrupt, already undone, already sinful, and craving corruption. *"For I was born a sinner—yes, from the moment my mother conceived me"* (Ps. 51:5 NLT). We find several accounts in the Bible of this degenerated nature of man full of corruption, such as:

> *"For out of the heart come evil thoughts—murder, adultery, sexual immorality, theft, false testimony, slander"* (Matt. 15:19 NIV).

> *"For from within, out of the heart of men, proceed the evil thoughts, fornications, thefts, murders, adulteries, deeds of coveting and wickedness, as well as deceit, sensuality, envy, slander, pride and foolishness"* (Mark 7:21-22 KJV).

The Word of God is stated as this from the old:

"Woe to those who plan iniquity, to those who plot evil on their beds! At morning's light they carry it out because it is in their power to do it" (Mic. 2:1 KJV).

"Even on their beds they plot evil; they commit themselves to a sinful course and do not reject what is wrong" (Ps. 36:4 KJV).

"Their feet rush into sin; they are swift to shed innocent blood. They pursue evil schemes; acts of violence mark their ways" (Isa. 59:7 KJV).

And finally:

"Be not deceived; God is not mocked: for whatsoever a man soweth that shall he also reap. For he that soweth to his flesh shall of the flesh reap corruption; but he that soweth to the spirit shall of the spirit reap life everlasting" (Gal. 6:7 KJV).

What we reap what we sow; it becomes our fruit for carnality breeds corruption, enmity begat hate, and transgression bestows offense. The only escape is God for sin separates us all from God.

For example, Jacob deceived his father. He took the skin of a kid and put it on himself. And when his blind father, Isaac, felt of him, he was hairy like his brother Esau for Esau was a hairy man. So, when the blind father felt the hair that was like Esau, he said he was Esau. Isaac had intended to bless his eldest son, Esau, but it was Jacob who received it. Jacob took through trickery his brother's birthright. And Esau sold his blessing for a bowl of porridge

(Gen. 27:41). But Jacob, a deceiver, a liar, and a thief was loved by God, redeemed and restored unto His righteousness.

> *For [the children] being not yet born, neither having done any good or evil, that the purpose of God according to election might stand, not of works, but of him that calleth;) It was said unto her, The elder shall serve the younger. As it is written, Jacob have I loved, but Esau have I hated. What shall we say then? [Is there] unrighteousness with God? God forbid. For he saith to Moses, I will have mercy on whom I will have mercy, and I will have compassion on whom I will have compassion. As it is written, Jacob have I loved, but Esau have I hated. (God's Sovereign choice).* Rom. 9:11-15 KJV.

Allow me to share more examples throughout mankind for clarity both biblical and historical:

Biblical accounts:

- o David slew a man to hide his transgression. And the prophet said, *"Now therefore the sword shall never depart from your house; because you have despised me, and have taken the wife of Uriah the Hittite to be your wife"* (2 Sam. 12:10).

- o Haman built a gallows for Mordecai, but Haman was hanged on Mordecai's gallows (Esther 7:10 KJV).

Historical Accounts:

- o Maxentius built a bridge (the Milvian Bridge) to drown Constantine, and he drowned himself crossing his own phony bridge. (Nixon, Rodgers, & Mynors 2015).

- o Tamerlane made a great iron cage in which to place Bajazet, and Tamerlane took Bajazet and kept him in that iron cage until he died. (Haaren, & Poland 2020).

- o Henry III of France was stabbed to death in the same room where he plotted the infamous massacre of the first Protestants (Mansfield 2012).

- o Pope Alexander VI was poisoned by a wine he made for another. (Laughlin 1907).

- o Marie Antoinette, on that gorgeous bridal procession through the streets of Paris to Notre Dame when she has married Louis XVI of France, gave orders to her soldiers to go up and down the procession as well as go outside and send away all of the ragged and the poor and the crippled. A few years later, down the same street she was carried, bound, to an executioner's court. (Knolles 1638, 220-221)

Chapter 5

IF THE LAW OF GOD IS TERRIBLE, THEN WHAT BREAKS IT?

"For to *be carnal minded is death*" (Rom. 8:6a KJV).

"*If ye live after the flesh, ye shall die: but if ye through the Spirit do mortify the deeds of the body, ye shall live*" (Rom. 8:13 KJV).

The unregenerate man is doomed. What shall he do? Where shall he turn? Who can break that awful chain? In the eighth chapter of the book of Romans, Scripture states: *"There is therefore now no condemnation to them which are in Christ Jesus, who walk not after the flesh, but after the Spirit. For the law of the Spirit of life in Christ Jesus has made me free from the law of sin and death"* (Rom, 8:1-2). This means that Christ Jesus has made me and you free from sin; He has broken the chain of the law of sin and death. As the passage continues:

> *For what the law could not do, in that it was weak through the flesh* (you and I), *God sending his own Son* (Jesus the Christ) *in the likeness of sinful flesh* (such as you and I), *and for* (our) *sin, condemned sin in the flesh* (broke that terrible chain). *That the righteousness of the law might be fulfilled in us who walk not after the flesh, <u>but after the Spirit</u>. For they that are after the flesh do mind* (care more for) *the things of the flesh, but they that are after the Spirit,* (care more for) *the things of the Spirit.* (Rom. 8:3-5)

Friends, it only took one death to break man's bondage, and that death is of Jesus the Son of God.

Therefore, what is the flesh? Merriam-Webster's Dictionary categorizes the flesh as a noun, and we understand that a noun is a person, place, or thing (Merriam-Webster Dictionary 2020). (please note that I have added the scripture verses for clarity):

1) The body, as distinguished from the mind and soul (mankind). Example: *"My spirit shall not always strive with man, for that he also is flesh"* (Gen. 6:3).

2) Human nature. Example:: *"The word was made flesh and dwelt among us"* (John 1:14).

3) Carnality; corporeal appetites. Example: *"The flesh lusteth against the spirit"* (Gal. 5:17).

4) A carnal state; a state of unrenewed nature. Example: *"They that are in the flesh cannot please God"*.

5) The corruptible body of man, or corrupt nature. Example: *"Flesh and blood cannot inherit the kingdom of God"* (1 Cor. 15:50).

Underlying all activity of the flesh is its opposition and hatred of God. *"After the flesh"* (Rom. 8 4-5) and *"in the flesh"* (Rom. 8:8-9) both describe that human nature is corrupt, directed, and under the control of sin. On the other hand, *"after the Spirit"* (Rom. 8:4-5), and *"in the Spirit"* (Rom. 8:9) offer the same effect as one being under the control of and conditioned to the Holy Spirit. Having *"the mind of the flesh"* (Rom. 8:5) is to have the things of the flesh as the preoccupation of thought, interest, affection, and purpose. *"The mind of the flesh"* includes the cognitive activities of reason, the emotional responses, and the personal volition controlled by the sinful flesh. *"The things of the Spirit," "after the Spirit," "in the Spirit," "the mind of the Spirit," "walking in the Spirit," and "after the Spirit"* contradicts this with completely different principles. It is desirous to be under the habitual control of the Holy Spirit.

The outcome of both principles is also very clear. *"The mind of the flesh is death"* (Rom.8:6). It has the effect of separation from God. The verse continues saying, *"the mind of the Spirit is life and peace."* The latter produces a relationship with God. When we are at one with God, we experience His love and peace. The opposite of enmity and death is reconciliation. Therefore, if you be in Christ, you're dead to sin (do not practice sin), for the Spirit of life is the Spirit of righteousness. And the Spirit of life in a man forever breaks that awful and welded chain, for the law of the Spirit of life has made us free from the law of sin and death. The Word of God draws us unto the will and obedience to Christ's abundant way of life which declares we walk in the freedom of life from the law.

Our spirit and flesh are in constant war with each other, and the only way we can be at peace is to walk in Christ. You see, we are spirit and flesh joined together. Our spirit and flesh make up our one being for our time on earth. In the English Standard Bible Version, it states: *"Watch and pray that you may not enter into temptation. The spirit indeed is willing, but the flesh is weak"* (Matt. 26:41). We know that our flesh fails us time and time again because, as Jesus said in the Scripture, we do not *"deny"* it. *"Then he said to the crowd, 'If any of you wants to be my follower, you must turn from your selfish ways, take up your cross daily, and follow me'"* (Luke 9:23 NLT). The flesh does not conquer the spirit. The flesh is weak, as Jesus said, and the flesh is a stumbling block to our spirit. That is why the mind that focuses on human nature is hostile toward God. It refuses to submit to the authority of God's law because it is powerless to do so.

I found that when people try to escape their destiny, meaning the Christian walk of life, they find themselves doing the same thing as Saul did, kicking against the prick. The spirit of oppression comes in many forms as it perpetuates an illusion of self-conceitedness. However, there's a small, still, peaceful voice that if we listen to will encourage, build, motivate our every thought unto a way of righteousness, though only if you allow your flesh to die to its desires. The spirit man is where we need to stand.

> *"I am the way, the truth, and the life: no man cometh unto the Father but by me"* (John 14:6 KJV).

> *"The Lord hath appeared of old unto me, saying, Yea, I have loved thee with an everlasting love: therefore, with lovingkindness have I drawn thee"* (Jer. 31:3 KJV).

Let's look at this closer, examining the story of Nicodemus, a man of the Pharisees, a member of the Jewish ruling council, and a learned and religious man who came by night to see and speak with Jesus the Rabbi (John 1:1-2 KJV).

Nicodemus: Whom Do You Seek?

Why did Nicodemus seek Jesus by night? Was it because he could not escape the pressures of his mind, his prestige, his position, his wealth, his knowledge, or was it just to avoid the hostility of his colleagues? Nicodemus knew he could not speak to Jesus by day for he did not want to lose his existence, pride, and acceptance in a society that dictated every move and thought of his being, wealth, and success (the flesh). I can see that he knew he had to answer his questions of doubt concerning the Rabbi once and for all. Was he the Christ?

We should give Nicodemus credit since he knew Jesus was not the product of any rabbinical school for His miracles marked Him as a prophet and distinguished Him from all who were guided merely by their belly and greed. However, Nicodemus knew the effect of Christ's miracles and how that the miracles proved that He who works them is from God (Acts 10:38). However, Nicodemus took a chance and, after speaking with this Rabbi, he finally succumbed to the thought, "How can I be born again?"

What may Nicodemus have felt at that moment? Was it excitement in finally meeting the Godman, the Rabbi, or was it pain and frustration with his training and the traditions of his faith in the God of his fathers? Or was he embarrassed, not wanting his fellow continuants to see him speaking to this man or even being interested in His way of life? You know how we act sometimes, wanting Jesus but not wanting Him more than our silly reputations, egotism, or self-importance.

Yet, after speaking with this Rabbi, Nicodemus was not satisfied with what he had heard. It wasn't the fact that he did not understand fully or believe; it was that he found himself barred forever from the kingdom by an impossible requirement, trapped like a mouse in a mousetrap seeking rescue. Nicodemus found his mind was in bondage, chained to and controlled by the rudiments of man's doctrine. As he tried to break free of his position, he found he was still a slave to the thoughts, traditions, experiences, position, training, prestige, and theology of who the Almighty God is. If only he could escape the devices of his flesh to take hold of what Jesus Christ was offering him, the new birth, the new life through Him. Many, like my brother Nicodemus, must learn God asks of us nothing impossible, for Christ's yoke *"is easy and my burden is light"* (Matt. 11:30 NIV).

Can you imagine Nicodemus's fight—the daily struggle between the spirit man warring with the natural man? It is the same battle we are struggling with and yet God has made an escape; that is through Jesus Christ. *"For God so loved the world that He gave His only begotten son for whosoever believe in Him should not perish but have everlasting life"* (John 3:16 KJV). Like Nicodemus, we allow our foolish pride to stop us from obtaining this freedom. We refuse to step down from our ivory tower of conceit and our dysfunctional way of life; we allow our status, title, position, or financial worth to cheat us from the very existence of Christ. Just as Nicodemus did, we walk away in sorrow for even our self-loathing cannot soothe the emptiness we feel Through the struggle, trials, and tribulation of life, we yearn to grasp hold of the teachings, and –some finally adhere, just as Nicodemus succumbed to the Spirit of the Lord Jesus Christ with supplication and joy.

But some refuse to receive this life of joy and everlasting peace for they hold on to a mirage that is full of pride, position, power, and wealth. We can look to Jesus's story to the people:

> *And he spake a parable unto them, saying, The ground of a certain rich man brought forth plentifully: And he thought within himself, saying, What shall I do, because I have no room where to bestow my fruits? And he said, This will I do: I will pull down my barns and build greater; and there will I bestow all my fruits and my goods. And I will say to my soul, Soul, thou hast much goods laid up for many years; take thine ease, eat, drink, and be merry. But God said unto him, Thou fool, this night thy soul shall be required of thee: then whose shall those things be, which thou hast provided? So is he that layeth up treasure for himself and is not rich toward God. Luke 12:16-21, KJV.*

You see, it is not how long it takes for you to say "yes" to God's will, but rather when you finally come to the end of yourself. It is then you will see. Luke 12:29-31 instructs:

> *And seek not ye what ye shall eat, or what ye shall drink, neither be ye of doubtful mind. For all these things do the nations of the world seek after: and your Father knoweth that ye have need of these things. But rather seek ye the kingdom of God; and all these things shall be added unto you.*

Many people struggle with what they have done, past or present, and never taking ahold of the "now". "Now faith is the substance of things hope for and the evidence of things not seen"

(Heb. 11:1 KJV). As I sit here thinking, so many questions come to mind. Even as I ponder on all the reasons, excuses, and not wanting to give up self, I cannot help but ask you, will you take ahold of Christ or will you allow your flesh to rob you of your wealth, your victory, and that more abundantly? What is holding you back? What is stopping you from taking a strong grip on the foundation of truth which is that Christ gives us life and all that more abundantly? Is it your excuses, your faults, your pretenses, or YOU?

I must ask if you are truly looking for a way out of your non-existent life or are you trying to find an easy way to obtain Christ without giving up your selfish, inconsistent life of loneliness, despair, depression, and your self-defeating attitudes? Do you find yourself trying to come unto Christ by way of trickery? Or maybe you feel if you can just slide into the mere presence of God, you will overcome this lifeless feeling of worthlessness. Do you go through the motions of being a Christian just to say, Look at me, see what I am doing, I'm a good person. Watch you are not fulfilling 2 Timothy 3:5: *"Having a form of godliness, but denying the power thereof: from such turn away."*

I have been there, being tossed to and from by the enemy's devices of self-allusion and a false sense of living. I have stood not understanding my purpose or place, reaching, never obtaining; fighting, never winning; crawling, yet struggling; crying out, "Help me, I've fallen." You are not alone when you find yourself continuing in these self-destructive acts of no return, looking to friends, co-workers, pastors, and prophets for the answers when you know, just as Nicodemus knew, *"You must be born again"* (John 3:7). That is not my way, but the way of Christ, not my thinking but the thinking of Christ, not my walk but the walk of God. I'm not preaching a mere cliché, saying "What would Jesus do," but challenging you to a complete transformation of thought, action, and deed. The Scripture states: *"there is a way which seemeth right unto a man, but the end thereof are the ways of death"* (Prov. 14:12).

Let's look at our current collective walk with God. As children of the Most High God, our personal relationship with Him is a journey of fulfillment, enlightenment, discernment, and wisdom. God endows us with spiritual, natural, and practical knowledge that governs our everyday lives. In our spiritual journey with God, He wants us to come to Him with humility. He doesn't want any unwanted sins to enter in. He commands us to leave worldly concerns and focus on Him by being obedient to His commandments and worshipping Him. In the book of Mark, we see such a case, as Christ empowered His disciples for their journey of righteousness by traveling light and keeping their minds focused on the task at hand.

> *And he called unto him the twelve, and began to send them forth by two and two; and gave them power over unclean spirits; And commanded them that they should take nothing for their journey, save a staff only; no scrip, no bread, no money in their purse: But be shod with sandals; and not put on two coats. And he said unto them, In what place <u>soever</u> ye enter into an house, there abide till ye depart from that place. And whosoever shall not receive you, nor hear you, when ye depart thence, shake off the dust under your feet for a testimony against them. Verily I say unto you, It shall be more tolerable for Sodom and Gomorrha in the day of judgment, than for that city. And they went out and preached that men should repent. And they cast out many devils, and anointed with oil many that were sick, and healed them* Mark 6:7-13.

Christ has and continues to prepare us all to represent Him in winning souls for His kingdom. However, that can only be done if we have the right mindset by always concerning ourselves with the affairs of the Kingdom. It is our thoughts, deeds, actions, and beliefs that serve as a signpost as to what type of Christians we are to the unbeliever. Are we the type of Christians who arrogantly wear our faith on our sleeves and expect others to go down and worship us? Do we let pride, vanity, and the cravings of power within the body of Christ get in the way of being effective leaders, ambassadors, and disciples for the glorification of His kingdom? *"For there is a man whose labour is in wisdom, and in knowledge, and in equity; yet to a man that hath not laboured therein shall he leave it for his portion. This also is vanity and a great evil"* (Eccles 2:21).

Are we humble servants who strive to live a life of integrity, holiness, and godliness? Do we see ourselves doing the will of God with an approach of love, gratitude, humility, kindness, and empathy for the plight of those around us? Are we pew-sitters or strong advocates laying a strong spiritual foundation for the usher in the kingdom of God? *"But seek ye first the kingdom of God, and his righteousness; and all these things shall be added unto you"* (Matt 6:33).

Let's stop here for a minute and go before the throne of God Almighty for help, direction, and a complete transformation. Let's make it personal by praying together:

> *Father, King of Kings and Lord of Lords, the Great and Awesome God, the Mighty and Loving Savior, forgive me and have mercy, help and deliver me from my selfish ways and allow me to use what you have given me to truly build the kingdom of God rather than tearing it down. Allow my hands, feet, and mouth to*

strengthen and encourage. Allow my eyes to rejoice in the beauty of your Word. Father, give me life and that more abundantly and let my words and my mouth be an acceptable savor to your ears. Father, I beseech thee in the name of your Son, Jesus Christ. Amen

Chapter 6

THE CALL

In our journey with Christ Jesus, He has endowed every one of us with gifts of the spirit—some prophesying, some the gift of healing, some speaking in tongues, with others endowed with the ability to teach, pastor, evangelize, and lead apostleship. *("And he gave some, apostles; and some, prophets; and some, evangelists; and some, pastors and teachers; For the perfecting of the saints, for the work of the ministry, for the edifying of the body of Christ"* (Eph. 4:11-12 KJV.) Through these gifts, each of us has been mandated with a specific task to utilize these skills and attributes in the edification of His kingdom. *"Even so ye, forasmuch as ye are zealous of spiritual gifts, seek that ye may excel to the edifying of the church"* (1 Cor. 14:12).

Many of us have been called by God and entrusted with specific duties within the church. Some of us have been chosen as elders, evangelists, prophets, apostles, teachers, and pastors. We must be sure of our calling by seeking God through faithful prayer, supplication, and fasting. It would be a tragic mistake trying to second guess God on how, where, and when He will use us for the glorification of His kingdom. What we have achieved and done in our ministries is the results of all God has given us and not because of what we've achieved ourselves; it is God doing the increase.

> *I planted, Apollos watered, but God was causing the growth. So then neither the one who plants nor the one who waters is anything, but God who causes the growth. Now he who plants and he who waters are one; but each will receive his own reward according to his own labor. For we are God's fellow workers; you are God's field, God's building.* 1 Corinthians 3:6-9 KJV

When we remove ourselves from the will of God, we become self-centered and self-serving in the ministries we have either established or inherited. The Christ within us is bigger than anything we aspire to be or try to do. Taking credit for an accomplishment is outside of His will. *"Therefore pride compasseth them about as a chain; violence covereth them as a garment"* (Ps. 73:6).

Some are jealous of the God within you because you aspire to be like God. But some have no desire, nor have they reached a personal relationship in life with Christ. They only use Christ as *"having a form of godliness but denying the power thereof"* (2 Timothy 3:5a KJV), in the wrong possible way. You don't want to be Christ-like in thought, deed, or action, rather holding yourself in lofty positions with a haughty attitude. For this quest for a position, you become abusive, and you act more like agents of Satan than God Almighty. *"Set thou a wicked man over him: and let Satan stand at his right hand"* (Ps. 109:6). Remember is fallen because he tried to challenge the very authority of Yahweh because he wanted to be God himself. *"And he said unto them, I beheld Satan as lightning fall from heaven"* (Luke 10:18). Many who hold lofty titles in the church have fallen though are too arrogant and self-centered to see the errors of their way. *"Who can understand his errors? cleanse thou me from secret faults"* (Ps. 10:12). Are you one who has pursued the lust of the flesh and the pride of life to govern your decision-making process? Have you done unconscionable acts, such as adultery, homosexuality, vilifying members of the congregation, robbing the church treasury, and turning your back to the poor? Be forewarned: *"They are vanity, and the work of errors: in the time of their visitation they shall perish"* (Jer. 10:15).

There are those of you who believe the path of righteousness is to pursue the vanities of this world and to justify that it is the will of God. As the elect in the body of Christ, we must separate ourselves from the affairs of the world if we are to serve Christ our Lord. *"Teaching us that, denying ungodliness and worldly lusts, we should live soberly, righteously, and godly, in this present world"* (Titus 21:12). The Holy Bible gives us a ready blueprint of how church leadership should govern and carry themselves when doing the will of God, serving the needs of the body of Christ.

> *This is a true saying, If a man desire the office of a bishop, he desireth a good work. A bishop then must be blameless, the husband of one wife, vigilant, sober, of good behaviour, given to hospitality, apt to teach; Not given to wine, no striker, not greedy of filthy lucre; but patient, not a brawler, not covetous; One that ruleth well his own house, having his children in subjection with all gravity; (For if a man know not how to rule his own house, how shall he take care of the church of God?) Not a novice, lest being lifted up with pride he fall into the condemnation of the devil. Moreover he must have a good report of them which are without; lest he fall into reproach and the snare of the devil. Likewise must the deacons be grave, not double tongued, not given to much wine, not greedy of filthy lucre; Holding the mystery of the faith in a pure conscience. And let these also first be proved; then let*

them use the office of a deacon, being found blameless. Even so must their wives be grave, not slanderers, sober, faithful in all things. Let the deacons be the husbands of one wife, ruling their children and their own houses well. For they that have used the office of a deacon well purchase to themselves a good degree, and great boldness in the faith which is in Christ Jesus. 1 Timothy 1:1-13)

Therefore, my brothers and sisters in Christ Jesus, we must guard our walk with God at all times and deny our flesh daily to serve him. Our calling and the spiritual gifts God have given us are not to be taken lightly

> *"And he said to them all, If any man will come after me, let him deny himself, and take up his cross daily, and follow me"* (Luke 9:23, KJV).

> *"For the gifts and calling of God are without repentance"* (Rom. 11:29 KJV).

We don't have the right as leaders in the church to do what we please because our actions have terrible consequences for ourselves and the congregations we serve. No amount of earthly power, prestige, or honor can replace the presence of God in our lives. The abuse of our offices does not serve the image of the church well in the eyes of nonbelievers. In these last and final days, we must be proponents of the faithful by preparing the body elect for the trials and tribulations repeatedly foretold in the Word of God.

> *And Jesus answered and said unto them, Take heed that no man deceive you. For many shall come in my name,*

saying, I am Christ; and shall deceive many. And ye shall hear of wars and rumours of wars: see that ye be not troubled: for all these things must come to pass, but the end is not yet. For nation shall rise against nation, and kingdom against kingdom: and there shall be famines, and pestilences, and earthquakes, in divers places. All these are the beginning of sorrows. Then shall they deliver you up to be afflicted and shall kill you: and ye shall be hated of all nations for my name's sake. And then shall many be offended, and shall betray one another, and shall hate one another. And many false prophets shall rise and shall deceive many. And because iniquity shall abound, the love of many shall wax cold. But he that shall endure unto the end, the same shall be saved. And this gospel of the kingdom shall be preached in all the world for a witness unto all nations; and then shall the end come.
Matthew 24:5-14

Where do you stand my brothers and sisters who have been called by God to serve and do His will? Do you stand with Him or with the bright lights and big cities of the world? Do you seek fame and fortune and try to justify it in the name of Christ Jesus or will you be that rare exception and seek the kingdom of God by obeying His commandants, tending to the spiritual needs of the flock, and helping both the poor and widowed? Be the ambassador of Christ that God has mandated you to be and both you and your ministries will flourish for His sake. Our journey with God will be one of self-fulfillment and victorious living in these uncertain times!

Chapter 7

Deceptive Faith and Counterfeit Works

There is a spirit of malcontent in the land. It projects a false attribute of faith that is not of God. It deceives many and is a spiritual stronghold that the body of Christ has allowed manifesting through the allusion of grandeur. It is evil, destructive, and unholy in its intent. Its representatives flaunt its mode of operation with their allegiance to The Great Apostasy or falling away. This falling away is a criminal enterprise that misplaces the glory of God within those who worship self-gratification. The pursuit of self has a bright light and big city mentality at the expense of all who fall trap to its dainties. The mirage of false worship, false faith, and counterfeit works have become the rule of society, especially for those who dress their flesh in a garment of sedition and compromise. Some have even gone as far as making the art of giving, encouraging, and loving others under the pretense of gaining prestige, position, glory, and profit. Society accepts this behavior of doing as you want and yet professing Christianity though you destroy every member at the expense of God's lambs.

Ecclesiastes 1:19 declares, *"The thing that hath been, it is that which shall be; and that which is done is that which shall be done:*

and there is no new thing under the sun." What Solomon implies with these words is that there is nothing we can hide from God. He has seen all manners of pretense, deceptive faith, and counterfeit works. He knows the naked roots of appeasement and the compromise of one's faith and good works for fleshly desires. Many do so at such a trifling extent that they affect a spiritual con job on God Almighty. How can you identify people with deceptive faith and counterfeit works? Let's examine what the Word of God says about individuals with phony faith.

> What doth it profit, my brethren, though a man say he hath faith, and have not works? can faith save him? If a brother or sister be naked, and destitute of daily food, And *one of you say unto them, Depart in peace, be ye warmed and filled; notwithstanding ye give them not those things which are needful to the body; what doth it profit? Even so faith, if it hath not works, is dead, being alone. Yea, a man may say, Thou hast faith, and I have works: shew me thy faith without thy works, and I will shew thee my faith by my works. Thou believest that there is one God; thou doest well: the devils also believe, and tremble. But wilt thou know, O vain man, that faith without works is dead? Was not Abraham our father justified by works, when he had offered Isaac his son upon the altar? Seest thou how faith wrought with his works, and by works was faith made perfect? And the scripture was fulfilled which saith, Abraham believed God, and it was imputed unto him for righteousness: and he was called the Friend of God. Ye see then how that by works a man is justified, and not by faith only. Likewise also was not Rahab the harlot justified by works, when she had received the messengers,*

and had sent them out another way? For as the body without the spirit is dead, so faith without works is dead also. James 2:16-26 KJV

The Bible is clear about what constitutes true faith and what does not. In the old days of both the Old and New Testaments, the scribes, Pharisees, and Sadducees regularly gained influence and positions of and authority. Their faith was measured by their public display of works. This took the form of fasting in the public square, praying loudly for the crowds to hear, and giving alms to the poor as a symbolic gesture. That is why Christ called them hypocrites, vipers, and sons of Satan. They had as much faith as the man on the moon. Newsflash, nothing has changed since the crucifixion, resurrection, and glorification of our blessed Savior, Jesus Christ.

The body of believers in the church has assumed the same mindset of the Pharisees and Sadducees. We have leaders and members whose supposedly good works are only done so they can be seen by the parishioners. They are the ones given praise for the number of their tithes, the clothes they cars they drive, the jobs they hold, and the houses they live in. Meanwhile, parishioners who have given all they can afford in tithes are ridiculed and talk about because what they have offered does not meet the false ones' standards. Yes, they don't have fancy possessions or large bank accounts, however, they do have genuine faith and love of God. Still, those in authority don't see that genuine faith because they are too focused on satisfying their fleshly desires. Malcolm X was right when he said, "If you're are not careful, the newspapers will have you hating the people who are being oppressed and loving the people who are doing the oppressing" (Breitman 1971, 93). *"Let no man deceive you by any means: for that day shall not come, except there come a falling away first, and that man of sin be revealed, the son of perdition"* (2 Thess. 2:3KJV).

Many well-meaning saints of God have been led astray from their walk with Christ because they have let anybody and everybody who professes to be "born again" come into their house (temple of God) and sup with them. They come with no anointing (which is Jesus the Christ), no direction, no word; they come only to steal, kill, and destroy the move of God in ministry both naturally and spiritually.

> *"Take heed that ye do not your alms before men, to be seen of them: otherwise ye have no reward of your Father which is in heaven"* (Matt. 6:1 KJV).

> *"And when thou prayest, thou shalt not be as the hypocrites are: for they love to pray standing in the synagogues and in the corners of the streets, that they may be seen of men. Verily I say unto you, They have their reward"* (Matt. 6:5 KJV).

> *"But when ye pray, use not vain repetitions, as the heathen do: for they think that they shall be heard for their much speaking"* (Matt. 6:7 KJV).

Den of Thieves

Every day we hear through various media outlets about financial institutions taking taxpayer money and people's houses in foreclosure and other financial misdeeds. These crimes have become so perverse that the Federal Government has stepped in to sue these financial institutions to legally retrieve money due back to the US taxpayers. I bring this up because similar is taking place in the house of God; it has become a den of thieves instead of a sanctuary for righteousness' sake.

> *"And Jesus went into the temple of God, and cast out all them that sold and bought in the temple, and overthrew the tables of the moneychangers, and the seats of them that sold doves, And said unto them, It is written, My house shall be called the house of prayer; but ye have made it a den of thieves"* (Matt. 21:12-13 KJV).

Yet every day there are some pastors, evangelists, and other church figures who preach a false doctrine of darkness to rob both God and His people. The message I bring forth is especially meant for them. *"Will a man rob God? Yet ye have robbed me. But ye say, Wherein have we robbed thee? In tithes and offerings"* (Mal. 3:8 KJV). These people do not think they are robbing God, but they fail to look when it comes to tithes and offerings. In many respects, tithes have become their golden calf because what was meant for the house of God they have taken to indulge their personal lives of luxury. The money from fundraisers, special collections, pastoral anniversaries, revivals, and holy convocations has gone into their pockets to fund the desires of the flesh while at the same time most of the congregation struggle daily to make ends meet on a limited budget. Look what it says in Deuteronomy about this:

> *"If a man be found stealing any of his brethren of the children of Israel, and maketh merchandise of him, or selleth him; then that thief shall die; and thou shalt put evil away from among you"* (Deut. 24:7 KJV).

People holding offices within the body of believers are more concerned about how they look at retreats and such than saving souls. Again, this is not a judgment call on those that are made righteous by God but to those who sodomize and strip the members in their church body. I am talking about those who make their grandiose entrance to have the masses praise and worship them as if they are deities. They believe their rituals and traditions of men hold them unscathed and unharmed as they rob and seduce the men and women of God. They rob God every day when they stand the pulpit preaching falsehoods of prosperity implying their members are not blessed unless they make a certain type of money, drive a luxury car, or live in a big house. States Job 12:6 KJV: *"The tabernacles of robbers prosper, and they that provoke God are secure; into whose hand God bringeth abundantly."*

The false doctrine they preach is one of mayhem, confusion, and lies. The pulpit has become a personal fiefdom of power for them. They glorify themselves instead of the body elect. They have poisoned the body elect with their reprobate minds. *"They profess that they know God; but in works they deny him, being abominable, and disobedient, and unto every good work reprobate"* (Titus 1:16 KJV). In all, in the eyes of God, they have become spiritually, morally, and naturally unfit to lead a congregation. They have become servants of Satan instead of children of the Most High God. *"Now as Jannes and Jambres withstood Moses, so do these also resist the truth: men of corrupt minds, reprobate concerning the faith." Thus sayeth the Lord* (2 Tim. 3:8 KJV).

I cry out as John the Baptist did in exposing what the church has become. In many respects, God has left the building because they have chosen to honor themselves instead of Him; it is their achievements and milestones.

Nowhere do they humble themselves and give God the glory for where they are today. Not one ounce of humility comes out of their mouths of perversion. Surely, their day of reckoning will come unless they change who they are in Christ Jesus. They have allowed iniquity to enter their hearts, minds, and soul. The spirit man is a corruptible influence. And, just as with Satan, they have used their position to consume, and destroy the flocks that God has entrusted them with for guarding their very soul salvation. Just has He done with the disobedient nation of Israel, God will curse their ministries and allow them to falter because of their wickedness.

> "Then said he unto me, This is the curse that goeth forth over the face of the whole earth: for every one that stealeth shall be cut off as on this side according to it; and every one that sweareth shall be cut off as on that side according to it. I will bring it forth, saith the LORD of hosts, and it shall enter into the house of the thief, and into the house of him that sweareth falsely by my name: and it shall remain in the midst of his house, and shall consume it with the timber thereof and the stones thereof" (Zechariah 5:3-4 KJV).

If you think your worldly pursuits which you justify in the name of God will get you into heaven, you are sadly mistaken, my brothers and sisters. It is written in 1Corintians 6:10 KJV, *"Nor thieves, nor covetous, nor drunkards, nor revilers, nor extortioners, shall inherit the kingdom of God."*

The Walking Dead

Do you understand that what is happening in the House of Worship is no different than what is happening in the outside world? Some people have been easily manipulated to hate the less fortunate because they have been coached to render adorations, accolades, and honor to those in positions of influence who seek power because of their earthly works.

> *"But there were false prophets also among the people, even as there shall be false teachers among you, who privily shall bring in damnable heresies, even denying the Lord that bough them, and bring upon themselves swift destruction:* (1 Pet. 2:1 KJV).

These folks want to have a rock star image with false Holy Ghost-filled groupies (imitators of Christ wearing a costume of Christianity). Their purpose is not about doing the will of God to usher in the Kingdom, but rather it is about themselves, their image, and alter egos. Saints become so star-struck that they fail to see the fruits of their evilness.) *"Thefts, covetousness, wickedness, deceit, lasciviousness, an evil eye, blasphemy, pride, foolishness"* (Mark 7:22 KJV).

These individuals bring in false teachings and damnable doctrine and advice that are contrary to the will of God but instead directed to the will of their bellies. What was once viewed and accepted as good is now bad, and what was bad is now good. *"Woe unto them that call evil good, and good evil; that put darkness for light, and light for darkness; that put bitter for sweet, and sweet for bitter!"* (Isa 5:20 KJV). They embrace darkness under the cover of being representatives of Christ's Kingdom. *"Which justify the wicked for reward, and take away the righteousness of the righteous from him!"* (Isa 5:23 KJV).

As a result, over time, the members in that sanctuary become a dead church because false teachings or a lack of thereof grab hold. Saints are no longer deepened in the pure and unadulterated Word of God. In other words, they have become the un-churched, which means a body of believers with no spiritual love of God or for God, but carry a lustful desire with a worldly and corrupt influence. The "walking dead" they are. *"They are the kind who worm their way into homes and gain control over gullible women, who are loaded down with sins and are swayed by all kinds of evil desires"* (2 Tim. 3:6 NIV).

In many respects, Satan becomes their master and they become puppets he directs into all lasciviousness of the belly, having no shame nor repentance.) *"Who being past feeling have given themselves over unto lasciviousness, to work all uncleanness with greediness"* (Eph. 4:19 KJV). These walking dead become naturally and spiritually rotten at the core. But they must watch. *"Therefore as the fire devoureth the stubble, and the flame consumeth the chaff, so their root shall be as rottenness, and their blossom shall go up as dust: because they have cast away the law of the LORD of hosts, and despised the word of the Holy One of Israel"* (Isa. 5:24 KJV).

These are the pretenders and holy con artists who have turned the house of God into an imperial kingdom of their own. As 2 Chronicles 21:13 ISV describes, *"Instead, you have lived like the kings of Israel by causing Judah and the inhabitants of Jerusalem to commit cultic sexual immorality—just like Ahab's dynasty did! And you've killed your brothers who were better than you—your own father's dynasty!"*). These men and women continue to utter words of witchcraft and sorcery which have neither meaning nor place in God's House. They have killed the word of God and held captive the Holy Spirit; the flow and move of God are neither present nor welcomed.

> *"Woe unto you, scribes and Pharisees, hypocrites! for ye are like unto whited sepulchres, which indeed appear beautiful outward, but are within full of dead men's bones, and of all uncleanness"* (Matt. 23:27 KJV)

They are dead-men walking within the walls of Jezebel., (Just as Jezebel and Ahab transformed to the rudiments of idolatry, many have succumbed to the lifestyle of servitude to a dead building; they are a congregation of a stiff-necked, uncircumcised, and stubborn generation who gives in to their fleshly desires of covetousness and lascivious greed. They are creatures of habit to sin. *"And he cried mightily with a strong voice, saying, Babylon the great is fallen, is fallen, and is become the habitation of devils, and the hold of every foul spirit, and a cage of every unclean and hateful bird"* (Rev. 18:2).

Christ teaches us that true faith and good works are spiritual and from the heart. They are an extension of our walk with our Creator because it is a demonstration of our humbleness and obedience to His will. Most importantly, total submission to God means living a life where our love for Him extends to our fellow man. Christ is an exemplary example of a perfected life that denied things of this world for the preference of the keys of the kingdom of God. To enter the kingdom of heaven, our walk with God must be sincere and uncompromising. Our actions dictate whether we serve God or man. Not everyone who professes they love God and live a Christ-like walk will make it in because faith and works are compromised by a haughty attitude, lust, and a thirst for power. The Bible is very clear within its message: **_faith without works is dead._**

> *Lay not up for yourselves treasures upon earth, where moth and rust doth corrupt, and where thieves break through and steal: But lay up for yourselves treasures in heaven, where neither moth nor rust doth corrupt, and where thieves do not break through nor steal: For where your treasure is, there will your heart be also.*
> Matthew 6:19-21 KJV

If members don't go along with the party, they are ridiculed over the pulpit. It is like a spotlight is directed at them. Saints, this is not of God but instead, it is an allegiance to man or an institution. That is not a demonstration of faith with works; it is a physical representation of pompous piousness, hubris, self-conceitedness, and destructive behavior that divides a congregation. True works help to build and solidify our faith.

> *"Enter ye in at the strait gate: for wide is the gate, and broad is the way, that leadeth to destruction, and many there be which go in thereat: Because strait is the gate, and narrow is the way, which leadeth unto life, and few there be that find it"* (Matt. 7:13-14 KJV).

Therefore, what are the attributes of our works? It is prayer, fasting, empathy, humility, love, abstaining from fleshly thoughts, and crucifying our flesh. It requires obeying God by following His commandments and living a holy and victorious lifestyle. I cannot understand why we need to have admiration and approval from the world when our walk with God completes us. There is no greater approval in the universe than from God himself.

> *"Now faith is the substance of things hoped for, the evidence of things not seen"* (Heb, 11:1).

What is representative of true faith and works? Both require obedience and adherence to the will of God naturally and spiritually. This means knowing God is truly a supernatural being who keeps His covenant with His children. Take the word substance, for example. The Merriam-Webster dictionary online defines substance as the "ultimate reality that underlies all outward manifestations and change." (Merriam-Webster 2020). In this context, the substance is the expectation that God will provide and rescue us from any calamity that befalls us. It represents a natural act or supernatural manifestation of God through hope and miracles that will be done.

> *"Through faith we understand that the worlds were framed by the word of God, so that things which are seen were not made of things which do appear"* (Heb. 11:3).

The evidence of things not seen is faith because it will be done. After all, He has not let us down or forsaken us. True faith is a continuance of our walk with the Almighty, knowing that no matter what trial or tribulation comes our way, we can call on Him to rescue us, place us in His bosom of protection, and reestablish us.

> *By faith Abel offered unto God a more excellent sacrifice than Cain, by which he obtained witness that he was righteous, God testifying of his gifts: and by it he being dead yet speaketh. By faith Enoch was translated that he should not see death; and was not found, because God had translated him: for before his translation he had this testimony, that he pleased God. By faith Noah, being warned of God of things not seen as yet, moved with fear, prepared an ark to the saving of his house; by the which he condemned the world, and became heir of the righteousness which is by faith. By faith Abraham, when he was called to go out into a place which he should after receive for an inheritance, obeyed; and he went out, not knowing whither he went. By faith he (Abraham) sojourned in the land of promise, as in a strange country, dwelling*

> *in tabernacles with Isaac and Jacob, the heirs with him of the same promise.* Hebrew 11:4-5, 7-9

> *"But without faith it is impossible to please him: for he that cometh to God must believe that he is, and that he is a rewarder of them that diligently seek him"* (Heb. 11:6).

Our faith and works are forged in the seasons of our lives. They build our spiritual resolve and serve as a reminder that only through Him can we be rescued. Saints, there is nothing you hide because God knows the intent within our hearts. When we do things for God from the base of our spiritual nature, such as tithing, fasting, praying, or witnessing for Christ Jesus, we do so unselfishly with the understanding that we put our ego on the back burner by crucifying our flesh daily. We do it with a pure heart.

> *"Every man according as he purposeth in his heart, so let him give; not grudgingly, or of necessity: for God loveth a cheerful giver. And God is able to make all grace abound toward you; that ye, always having all sufficiency in all things, may abound to every good work"* (2 Cor. 9:7-8).

If you go through the motions of false faith with an unchanged attitude or with a distorted view that it will edify or increase your ministry, prestige, or wealth, then God doesn't want anything from you. God knows the intent and sincerity of your prayers. If your faith and works are not genuine, God will not answer them. If what you do is not for the edification and glorification of His kingdom, then you are wasting your time going through the motions. It behooves you though to come to God with a humble, meek and surrendering spirit at all times. God is long-suffering with us however He hates sin and pride because they separate us from His will. He punishes those who are proud, arrogant, and spiteful who seek glory for themselves.

> *"Therefore it shall come to pass, that as all good things are come upon you, which the LORD your God promised you; so shall the LORD bring upon you all evil things, until he have destroyed you from off this good land which the LORD your God hath given you"* (Josh. 23:15).

God wants us to cleave unto Him and flee from sin by changing what is in our hearts.

> *"Search me, O God, and know my heart: try me, and know my thoughts: And see if there be any wicked way in me, and lead me in the way everlasting"* (Ps 139:23-24).

What Are the Fruits of Authentic Faith & Works?

Let's look at an example for clarity. We know the Bible story of Abraham and Isaac. Abraham was the father and Isaac the son (Gen. 22:1-19). In their story, Abraham was put to his most agonizing test, a trial in which he had to sacrifice his only son. *"Take your son, your only son, Isaac, whom you love, and go to the region of Moriah. Sacrifice him there as a burnt offering on one of the mountains I will tell you about"* (Gen. 22:2 NIV). God blessed Abraham for being obedient through the demonstration of his faith and works. In this case, Abraham was willing to use his son as a willing sacrifice unto the Lord. Abraham loved and trusted God. God rewarded Abraham for his due diligence of faith and good works by making him the father of many nations. We are the seed of Abraham. Being obedient to God means that when He tells us to go left we do not hesitate, question him, or try to outthink Him. Just as we expect our children to be obedient when we tell them to do something, we should be the same way with our Father in heaven. Looking into this story further, I find several points of interest:

- God promised Abraham that he would make a great nation of him through Isaac, which caused Abraham to trust and obey God.

- Abraham told his servants "we" will be back, meaning both he and Isaac would be returning. In this obedience and trust, Abraham must have believed (showing action) God would either provide a substitute sacrifice or would raise Isaac from the dead (Heb. 11:19 KJV).

- This incident foreshadows God's sacrifice of His only Son, Jesus Christ, on the cross at Calvary for the sins of the world. Truly God's great love required of Himself what He did not require of Abraham.

- Mount Moriah, where the event took place (the name means Jehovah Jireh-God will provide), was a prelude to where King Solomon built the first temple and even today, the Muslim shrine. The Dome of the Rock in Jerusalem stands on the site of the sacrifice of Isaac.

- Abraham's obedience was credited to him as righteousness.

True faith is both believing and knowing God will do exactly what He said He would do in His timing and way. God gives us what we need at the time, not needless wants and lusts that are not in the spirit of Christ Jesus. So, I ask, is your faith lacking? Do you go through the motion of works without substance or belief? Has your pride separated you from the love of God? If so, God expects you to make amends by casting away what was old and unacceptable in His sight and repent. God wants you to humble yourself before Him naturally and spiritually. *"If my people, which are called by my name, shall humble themselves, and pray, and seek my face, and turn from their wicked ways; then will I hear from heaven, and will forgive their sin, and will heal their land"* (2 Chron. 7:14).

Be bold and turn away from sin by surrendering yourself to Christ Jesus. To become a new man or woman in Christ demands total surrender on your part through the remission of sins by water baptism in the authority of His name, thus being anointed and filled with the Holy Ghost. That is a true testament of faith and evidence of good works. Trust in God to lead you to all understanding and lean not unto your own. Let God have His way through you by walking in your true faith. This faith comes by living a holy and victorious lifestyle. Will you be the one today to bring forth edification in His kingdom?

Chapter 8

TRYING TO BE SOMEBODY IN A NOBODY'S DEAD CHURCH

A subject has plagued my spirit-man for many years because I see a great falling away of the church and apostasy of the spirit man that celebrates Satan and his kingdom instead of the body of Christ. *"Let no man deceive you by any means: for that day shall not come, except there come a falling away first, and that man of sin be revealed, the son of perdition"* (2 Thess. 2:3 KJV). Many well-meaning saints of God have been led astray because they have let anybody come into their sanctuary claiming to be an evangelist, prophet, deacon, or whatever else they call themselves without first checking their credentials. Most importantly, they have failed to consult God Almighty. *"But there were false prophets also among the people, even as there shall be false teachers among you, who privily shall bring in damnable heresies, even denying the Lord that bought them, and bring upon themselves swift destruction"* (2 Pet. 2:1 KJV).

The Traits of a Spiritually Dead Church
(Note: church represents a body of believers – not a building.)

No Joyful Noise Unto the Lord

How many times have you walked into a building you believed was filled with believers, wanting to praise and worship God, only to have the person seated next to you attack your praise and worship? Didn't David make a joyful noise unto the Lord? *"Let us come before his presence with thanksgiving and make a joyful noise unto him with psalms"* (Ps. 95:2 KJV). The problem with some churchgoers today is that they have become so doctrine-bound, procedure-oriented, and ceremonial-, that they have purposely forgotten to praise God at every juncture.

They have misinterpreted Paul when he spoke on discipline in the church. Paul was referring to the body of Christ as a living and breathing organism that must have order so it can grow and mature. When God created the heavens and the universe, He gave order to the void. *"And the earth was without form, and void; and darkness was upon the face of the deep. And the Spirit of God moved upon the face of the waters"* (Gen. 1:2 KJV). Yet some congregations have interpreted the law in a physical sense, just as the Pharisees and Sadducees did when Christ had His ministry on earth as God manifested in the flesh. Therefore, it is not surprising that Paul said in 2 Cor. 3:6 KJV, *"Who also hath made us able ministers of the New Testament; not of the letter, but of the spirit: for the letter killeth, but the spirit giveth life."* So the next time the person seated next to you criticizes you, tell them you have a disease called the Holy Ghost Fire.

No Spirit of Repentance

Today, too many believers, it seems like anything goes. Men and women come to their place of worship in provocative clothing; they are told they can do whatever they desire as long as they pay their tithes. Some people are so bold they pass messages to each other's spouses relaying sexual innuendos, playing the numbers, setting up drug trades, etc. *"For whoremongers, for them that defile themselves with mankind, for menstealers, for liars, for perjured persons, and if there be any other thing that is contrary to sound doctrine"* (1 Tim. 1:10 KJV)." There shall be no such things as this in the house of God's worship.

The Bible is very explicit; sin is sin in the eyesight of God. *"O ye sons of men, how long will ye turn my glory into shame? how long will ye love vanity, and seek after leasing? Selah"* (Ps. 4:2 KJV). Somehow, we have forgotten to fear God out of reverence and respect. *"God is greatly to be feared in the assembly of the saints, and to be had in reverence of all them that are about him"* (Ps 89:7 KJV). There are times when people treat God as their homeboy instead of the Father who lovingly and gently disciplines us. Doesn't Proverbs 9:10 KJV tells us that: *"The fear of the LORD is the beginning of wisdom: and the knowledge of the holy is understanding?"* The next time you hear someone tells you that you don't have to repent for sin, either lovingly rebuke them or find another house of worship that is doctrinally sound.

False Edification of God's Kingdom

There is no greater threat to the saints of God than to have a puppeteer of Satan teaching unsound and undisciplined doctrine. *"The prophets prophesy falsely, and the priests bear rule by their means; and my people love to have it so: and what will ye do in the end thereof?"* (Jer. 5:31 KJV). You need to guard your spirit man by knowing the Word of God yourself, not allowing any man or woman to interpret it for you. That is why God commands us in 2 Timothy 2:15 KJV to *"Study to shew thyself approved unto God, a workman that needeth not to be ashamed, rightly dividing the word of truth."* There is another part of that scripture that is equally important that most saints forget to remember. *"But shun profane and vain babblings: for they will increase unto more ungodliness"* (2 Tim. 2:16 KJV).

That is right; flee from unsound doctrine. Did God not instruct us to flee from evil whenever we come across it? When God talks about fleeing, He is not telling us to run away like if you are escaping a pack of hungry wolves (it seems that many churches are full of them), but rather to be wise and able to discern unsound doctrine wherever Satan rears his ugly head.

Pride and Vanity

Pride and vanity are two sisters of evil. Do I need to mention Cain and Abel as proof of how pride, arrogance, jealousy, and vainness lead to death and destruction? God's judgment for those who are prideful is swift and quick. *"Thy terribleness hath deceived thee, and the pride of thine heart, O thou that dwellest in the clefts of the rock, that holdest the height of the hill: though thou shouldest make thy nest as high as the eagle, I will bring thee down from thence, saith the LORD"* (Jer. 49:16 KJV). Pride and envy make people do and say things uncharacteristic of their nature. It is a disease of hate, manipulation, and covertness. These twin sisters of evil cause wars, break marriages, destroy friendships, and demolish congregations.

Most depressing, though, is that pride and vanity are more prevalent in the church than in the outside world. People have become demonically obsessed with money, position, and power within the church. *"For unclean spirits, crying with loud voice, came out of many that were possessed with them: and many taken with palsies, and that were lame, were healed"* (Acts 8:7 KJV). Let's face it, some churches have become the den of the damned instead of a sanctuary for the Almighty because of the jealous intentions, misgivings, and physical ugliness displayed by some people (carnal Christians) in the house of God.

Unforgiving Spirit –

When the disciples of Christ asked how many times, we should forgive someone, he told them:

> *"Then came Peter to him, and said, Lord, how oft shall my brother sin against me, and I forgive him? till seven times? Jesus saith unto him, I say not unto thee, Until seven times: but, Until seventy times seven"* (Matt. 18:21 KJV).

With this said, why are the saints of God so unforgiving of their fellow brothers and sisters in the house of worship or even the street? Why is it that you can scream and shout "thank you, Jesus" during church, but later in the week have the spirit of Jezebel? *"But there was none like unto Ahab, which did sell himself to work wickedness in the sight of the LORD, whom Jezebel his wife stirred up"* (1 Kings 21:25). Didn't Christ command us to forgive our neighbor and even love our enemy? Matthew 5:44 commands, *"But I say unto you, Love your enemies, bless them that curse you, do good to them that hate you, and pray for them which despitefully use you, and persecute you."* How can you say you love Christ but hate your brother? Worst yet, how can you be judgmental and vindictive towards that person? Judging someone in a negative light is eternal damnation. *"Whosoever hateth his brother is a murderer: and ye know that no murderer hath eternal life abiding in him"* (1 John 3:15). Knowing this, how can you talk about that individual behind his back and say cruel and hurtful things? Don't you know the Bible's warning about an evil tongue is the spiritual equivalent to hate speech on your part? The Bible has much to say about an unbridled tongue.

> *Even so the tongue is a little member, and boasteth great things. Behold, how great a matter a little fire kindleth! And the tongue is a fire, a world of iniquity: so is the tongue among our members, that it defileth the whole body, and setteth on fire the course of nature; and it is set on fire of hell. For every kind of beasts, and of birds, and of serpents, and of things in the sea, is tamed, and hath been tamed of mankind: But the tongue can no man tame; it is an unruly evil, full of deadly poison. Therewith bless we God, even the Father; and therewith curse we men, which are made after the similitude of God. Out of the same mouth proceedeth blessing and cursing. My brethren, these things ought not so to be. (James 3:5-10)*

Do the right thing and forgive your neighbor. And if you have done wrong against someone, ask for their forgiveness. If they don't, that is on them. You humble yourself before God and ask for His forgiveness.

Contention, Disruption, and a Spirit of Rebellion –

How many times have you told your children to be quiet because you want some peace in your house? Don't you know that we disrupt the same way if we don't respect the man of God whom He has put over you to shepherd His flock? Some congregations have a God-fearing and loving pastor, but the members go out of their way to make his life miserable by not giving him the due respect he deserves. Don't you know contention, disruption, and rebellion are attributes of witchcraft? *"For rebellion is as the sin of witchcraft, and stubbornness is as iniquity and idolatry. Because thou hast rejected the word of the LORD, he hath also rejected thee from being king"* (1 Sam. 15:23 KJV). Don't you know that witchcraft and the spirit of rebellion is another Jezebel spirit? Read what it says in 2 Kings 9:22 KJV: *"And it came to pass, when Joram saw Jehu, that he said, Is it peace, Jehu? And he answered, What peace, so long as the whoredoms of thy mother Jezebel and her witchcrafts are so many?"* God wants us to be spiritually disciplined so we can receive the fulfillment of the Holy Spirit. However, we as saints of God need to have a teachable disposition. That won't happen if you can't be still so that the Holy Ghost can rain down upon you. Be obedient to the servant that God has entrusted to oversee his flock.

Lustfulness –

Some saints have trouble controlling the beast of the desire of the flesh. Lustfulness is not just about sex. You can lust after food, fast cars, and fine clothes. Lust is all about controlling your flesh. *"For the flesh lusteth against the Spirit, and the Spirit against the flesh: and these are contrary the one to the other: so that ye cannot do the things that ye would"* (Gal. 5:17 KJV). It is the lust of the flesh that separates us from the will and love of God. God commands us to crucify our flesh daily.

Yet in some of our churches, lust runs rampant like wildfire. It consumes and destroys ministries and congregations alike because there is a lack of Godly discipline among the leaders and church members. Man, in his carnal state, can never inherit the kingdom of God because of their worldly influence. The kingdom of God is not of this world's saints. *"For this ye know, that no whoremonger, nor unclean person, nor covetous man, who is an idolater, hath any inheritance in the kingdom of Christ and of God"* (Eph. 5:5 KJV). You must let go of the things of this world and submit to Christ Jesus. Mark 8:36 KJV questions, *"For what shall it profit a man, if he shall gain the whole world, and lose his own soul?"*

Anger –

The word anger conjures up violent images of willful destruction and chaos. Anger in the natural and spiritual sense is not far off the mark. When people get angry, they do and say destructive things without thinking about the situation though. Before long, it is too late to undo the damage that has been done. As stated in Psalm 37:8 KJV, *"Cease from anger, and forsake wrath: fret not thyself in any wise to do evil."* The Bible teaches us to think before we get angry so that we can see the error of our ways before we go off the deep end. *"Wherefore, my beloved brethren, let every man be swift to hear, slow to speak, slow to wrath"* (James 1:19 KJV).

However, some circumstances led us to anger if we let our spiritual guard down. How many times have you left church service feeling angry instead of having your spirit man refresh? If this is happening to you then either your spirit man is not right with God or you have a demonic stronghold in your sanctuary. If the church is not right with God, then the blessing of the Holy Spirit cannot permeate the body during service. People come in and leave with the same spirit they bought with them.

Some brothers and sisters won't let go of the bitterness are inside them. *"Let all bitterness, and wrath, and anger, and clamour, and evil speaking, be put away from you, with all malice"* (Eph. 4:31 KJV). There are times that the leaders in the church are sitting up in the pulpit themselves filled with anger and vindictiveness which they distribute to the flock. Always guard yourself with the whole armor of God. *"Wherefore take unto you the whole armour of God, that ye may be able to withstand in the evil day, and having done all, to stand"* (Eph. 6:13 KJV).

Gossip

There is no doubt the evil of gossip is a religious libel in every sense of the word. It is slander against your neighbor. Exod. 20:16 KJV *commands, "Thou shalt not bear false witness against thy neighbour."* Gossip is a religious hate speech against your neighbor, friends, and even enemies. The Bible is very clear when it comes to unwarranted gossip. *"He that hideth hatred with lying lips, and he that uttereth a slander, is a fool"* (Prov. 10:18 KJV). Yet in the church, gossip has taken on a new form of hypocrisy, even coming down from the pulpit to control, demean, and ridicule. Gossip is used in the church is as a cloak of maliciousness. *"As free, and not using your liberty for a cloke of maliciousness, but as the servants of God"* (1 Pet. 2:16 KJV). It is a tool of open warfare against the saints within the body of Christ by Satan's cohorts.

Many people have been turned away and left the church by harmful and hateful gossip directed at them by leadership within that fellowship. If you continually gossip about your brothers or sisters within the confines of your sanctuary and it's condoned by the leadership, then you need to check yourself and ask God and the person you've demeaned for forgiveness. Not doing so exposes you to the wrath of God. *"Whoso privily slandereth his neighbour, him will I cut off: him that hath an high look and a proud heart will not I suffer"* (Ps. 101:5 KJV). Most church people think that because God is long-suffering, He will not punish them. Please know that God is a balanced God in His love and wrath, and just as His love is great, His wrath is very harsh. *"Therefore is the anger of the LORD kindled against his people, and he hath stretched forth his hand against them, and hath smitten them: and the hills did tremble, and their carcasses were torn in the midst of the streets. For all this his anger is not turned away, but his hand is stretched out still"* (Isa. 5:25 KJV). He will bring the ministry of the so-called righteous leader when they lie, manipulate, and gossip to naught. You must repent because the kingdom of God is at hand. *"If they shall fall away, to renew them again unto repentance; seeing they crucify to themselves the Son of God afresh, and put him to an open shame"* (Heb. 6:6 KJV).

Lack of Spiritual Discipline-

Religious teaching and rhetoric have become candy-coated with no substance in some of today's churches. Church leaders are telling the saints what they want to hear and not preaching the pure, unadulterated word of God. *"For the time will come when they will not endure sound doctrine; but after their own lusts shall they heap to themselves teachers, having itching ears"* (2 Tim. 4:3 KJV). True holiness has been regulated to the sidelines, replaced with a false prosperity ministry based on unobtainable worldly influences. Saints are no longer instructed in how to discern the Word of God, how to fast and pray, and how to apply practical biblical applications to their everyday lives. Many pulpit leaders have cultivated a rock star image complete with groupies and an entourage.

Take for example the misinterpretation of the armor-bearer. The biblical description of the armour bearer was one anointed to help his master during times of major battles. *"And the men of the garrison answered Jonathan and his armourbearer, and said, Come up to us, and we will shew you a thing. And Jonathan said unto his armourbearer, Come up after me: for the LORD hath delivered them into the hand of Israel"* (1 Sam. 14:12 KJV).

The armourbearer was a trusted associate who was willing to die alongside his master. Today's equivalent of the armour bearer in the pulpit has become a flunky in many respects because they've helped reinforce the notion that church leadership is unapproachable by the average churchgoer. The members of the congregation work to curry favor, carrying leader's Bibles, fetching water for them to, wiping their brow, and following behind them like a puppy dog. They have no practical applicable purpose except to humiliate themselves to get closer to the pastor. It is no wonder that most parishioners are turned off by the religious instruction they are getting. In situations such as this, we need to call on the Holy Ghost to truly deepen our understanding of the word of God.

> *"Which things also we speak, not in the words which man's wisdom teacheth, but which the Holy Ghost teacheth; comparing spiritual things with spiritual"* (1 Cor. 2:13 KJV).

Many pastors have even gone so far to say there's no need to seek the Holy Ghost. They preach "do, no change, do not worry about your conviction, just continue to be who you are." Such doctrine is incorrect and blasphemous against God Almighty himself.

> *"Wherefore I say unto you, All manner of sin and blasphemy shall be forgiven unto men: but the blasphemy against the Holy Ghost shall not be forgiven unto men"* (Matt. 12:31 KJV).

> *"And he opened his mouth in blasphemy against God, to blaspheme his name, and his tabernacle, and them that dwell in heaven"* (Rev. 13:6 KJV).

God gives these cohorts of Satan to a reprobate mind because they have purposely strayed from his word, as cited in Romans 1:28 KJV: *"And even as they did not like to retain God in their knowledge, God gave them over to a reprobate mind, to do those things which are not convenient."* Their undisciplined lifestyle and teachings are like poisonous words to the saints of God. *"Their throat is an open sepulchre; with their tongues they have used deceit; the poison of asps is under their lips"* (Rom. 3:13 KJV). Again, the Bible is very specific in that we need to seek first the kingdom of God for righteousness's sake. We should live our lives in a disciplined approach focused on God as the center of our existence. That means practicing and applying godly virtues both naturally and spiritually.

Refusing to Tithe

Refusing to give back to God that which is righteously His is like stealing from the storehouse.

> *"Will a man rob God? Yet ye have robbed me. But ye say, Wherein have we robbed thee? In tithes and offerings. Ye are cursed with a curse: for ye have robbed me, even this whole nation"* (Mal. 3:8-9 KJV).

The problem is not so much that saints are refusing to tithe but what happens to the money after they do. Often the church has purposely overtaxed its members for unsound purposes. For example, the ever-elusive building fund that never seems to make repairs or additions to the sanctuary. The purpose of tithing was to take care of the poor, widowed, and orphaned. *"Pure religion and undefiled before God and the Father is this, to visit the fatherless and widows in their affliction, and to keep himself unspotted from the world"* (James 1:27 KJV). In many respects, church leaders have used the tithing money as an endless trough to feed their golden calf of self-indulgence. *"They have turned aside quickly out of the way which I commanded them: they have made them a molten calf, and have worshipped it, and have sacrificed thereunto, and said, These be thy gods, O Israel, which have brought thee up out of the land of Egypt"* (Exod. 32:8 KJV). They have spent vast sums on fancy cars, clothes, homes, and memberships to exclusive clubs. They have wined and dined themselves in adulterous affairs. In other words, they have robbed God with their vanity, selfishness, and wickedness.

> *"Behold, these are the ungodly, who prosper in the world; they increase in riches"* (Ps. 73:12 KJV).

Very little, if any, of parishioners' tithes are used for missionary work, aid the unfortunate, or minister to those who caught by the desires of the world, such as drugs, alcohol, or prostitution. I remember watching a church video of a congregation that was on a supposed mission to Puerto Rico. They became frightened because the assistant pastor had accidentally driven them into the wrong neck of the woods. If that was the case, why would they go on a mission in the first place? Their idea of missionary work was staying in some fancy hotel and doing public service work, like picking up litter, just to make a name for themselves. There was no mention of outreach at all. The Bible is very specific of what works, faith, and ministry is all about.

> *"My brethren, have not the faith of our Lord Jesus Christ, the Lord of glory, with respect of persons. For if there come unto your assembly a man with a gold ring, in goodly apparel, and there come in also a poor*

man in vile raiment; And ye have respect to him that weareth the gay clothing, and say unto him, Sit thou here in a good place; and say to the poor, Stand thou there, or sit here under my footstool: Are ye not then partial in yourselves, and are become judges of evil thoughts? Hearken, my beloved brethren, Hath not God chosen the poor of this world rich in faith, and heirs of the kingdom which he hath promised to them that love him? But ye have despised the poor. Do not rich men oppress you, and draw you before the judgment seats?" James 2:1-6 KJV.

God does not have time for us to play church with His people. It is a dangerous game. Most importantly, though, there are thousands of individuals who need to hear the Word of God for themselves because they have lost all hope in these last days. Pray and let God lead you to give your tithes and offerings to houses of worship that do His will with this money.

These are just a few characteristics of a dead church, but what happens if you believe in your heart that God has directed you to this place of fellowship? How do you know if God wants you to try to revive a church that is already on life support? There are situations where no amount of prayer, fasting, or revivals are going to revive that church unless the leadership and the congregants want it to happen. Sometimes in our zeal to change something for the better, we become, disillusioned, unfocused, and complacent in the same way as the spiritually dead. Eventually, we too become part of the same yellow wallpaper that has consumed the people of God within that spiritually dead church. I always like to use the Vietnam analogy in describing what should be done with a spiritually dead church; sometimes you have to destroy the village to save it.

Before putting yourself through taxing and consuming mission, you need to fast, pray, and seek out God to determine if He mandated your spirit man to change the religious mentality of the church or if you are just walking in your flesh. *"Knowing this, that the law is not made for a righteous man, but for the lawless and disobedient, for the ungodly and for sinners, for unholy and profane, for murderers of fathers and murderers of mothers, for manslayers"* (1Tim. 1:9 KJV).

Let's look at the other side of the coin. What about those churchgoers who refuse to grow in their walk with God by strengthening their faith and being nourished by the Holy Ghost? They prefer to operate in churches where the teaching is weak, the pastor is tired, and the music ministry is non-existent. This is the place where weak-minded saints will connive their way into positions of authority for prestige purposes and self-fulfillment of their fleshly desire. These saints become stuck in a spiritual time warp. They have bought in a stronghold where they can't go any further in their relationship with God because they are neither being taught nor deepened.

That same satanic malfeasance is transferred into them, which then they take to their homes and jobs. Their households become hellish and undisciplined. Marriages are broken because the husband is looking over the fence at the honey next door while the wife is midnight creeping with every Tom, Dick, and Harry. Their children are disrespectful and troublesome. These immature and carnal churchgoers become despondent about their predicament and call on the same improper leader to pray over them which does nothing but open them up to more attacks by demonic influences because they were never taught to use their weapons of spiritual warfare to fend off the enemy in the first place. *"Thy prophets have seen vain and foolish things for thee: and they have not discovered thine iniquity, to turn away thy captivity; but have seen for thee false burdens and causes of banishment"* (Lam 2:14 KJV). If you are morally degenerate, why would you want to distribute bad spirits upon the people that are in God's house? *"He that saith, I know him, and keepeth not his commandments, is a liar, and the truth is not in him"* (1 John 2:4 KJV).

The best way to guard your spirit man against developing a fatal attraction to dead and demonically oppressed churches is to seek God on all decisions both naturally and spiritually. You need to ask of Him for wisdom, discernment, and courage in making such a life or death decision. *"The LORD'S voice crieth unto the city, and the man of wisdom shall see thy name: hear ye the rod, and who hath appointed it"* (Micah 6:9 KJV). Why do I say a life or death situation? It's because wherever you choose to attend service it can have a direct bearing on your soul salvation. Going to a spiritually dead, morally corrupt, and demonically possessed church can do serious damage to your spirit man and your walk with God. Before it is all done and finish, you could become a spiritual casualty, uncertain of your walk with God. Remember Satan is both the author of confusion and deceit. *"For God is not the author of confusion, but of peace, as in all churches of the saints"* (1 Cor. 14:33 KJV).

God gives us free will because He knows that life's trials and tribulations will bring us back to Him. You can either choose the path of holiness and righteousness to govern your life or a life in the world's wilderness which will eventually lead to spiritual and natural death. Joshua said it best: *"And if it seem evil unto you to serve the LORD, choose you this day whom ye will serve; whether the gods which your fathers served that were on the other side of the flood, or the gods of the Amorites, in whose land ye dwell: but as for me and my house, we will serve the LORD"* (Josh. 24:15 KJV).

Chapter 9

WHAT DOES LOVE HAVE TO DO WITH IT?

If I could speak all the languages of earth and angels, but didn't love others, I would only be a noisy gong or a clanging cymbal. If I had the gift of prophecy, and if I understood all of God's secret plans and possessed all knowledge, and if I had such faith that I could move mountains, but didn't love others, I would be nothing. If I gave everything I have to the poor and even sacrificed my body, I could boast about it; [a] *but if I didn't love others, I would have gained nothing. Love is patient and kind. Love is not jealous or boastful or proud or rude. It does not demand its own way. It is not irritable, and it keeps no record of being wronged. It does not rejoice about injustice but rejoices whenever the truth wins out. Love never gives up, never loses faith, is always hopeful, and endures through every circumstance. Prophecy and speaking in unknown languages*[b] *and special knowledge will become useless. But love will last forever! Now our knowledge is partial and incomplete, and even the gift of prophecy reveals only part of the whole picture! But when full understanding comes, these partial things will become useless. When I was a child, I spoke and thought and reasoned as a child. But when I grew up, I put away childish things. Now we see things imperfectly as in a cloudy mirror, but then we will see everything with perfect clarity. [c] All that I know now is partial and incomplete, but then I will know everything completely, just as God now knows me completely. Three things will last forever—faith, hope, and love—and the greatest of these is love. (1 Corinthians 1-13 KJV)*

What does love cost and how much will it cost you for success, fame, and prestige? As I think about the physical aspect of love, I am reminded of both the title of Tina Turner's smash hit and the movie that was a living biography of life and hell with Ike Turner. Fame brought much glory and prestige to Tina, but also much pain and sorrow. Here we find a woman who was physically and verbally abused, yet this is typical of what many couples are experiencing in some marriages today worldwide. Tina Turner was raped, beaten until she was half-dead, and demeaned verbally in every possible way.

The reason that I bring up the life of Tina Turner is that it is typical of both the famous and infamous trying to seek love in objects, emotions, and destructive habits like drug and alcohol abuse. But that is infamous; what about you who are the broken, beaten, and downtrodden of the world? Does this describe you too?. Some call it the American dream: the wife/husband, 1.5 children, big house with a white picket fence, and the exceptional job that brings power and authority. However, Paul tells us in 1 Corinthians 13: 1-13 that we can have all the talents and abilities in the world, but without love they mean nothing. In Luke 10:27, we find Christ's greatest commands which are *"you must love the Lord your God with all your heart, all your soul, all your strength, and all your mind"* and *'Love your neighbor as yourself."* In John 3:16, it states that *"God so loved the world that he gave his only, begotten Son and that whoever believes in him shall have everlasting life."*

What is this love that Paul expounds and why is it so elusive to some? First and foremost, let's look at how Paul portrays love. Is this love physical or spiritual that he speaks of? Love is a verb that denotes the act of doing something. Hence, we find that Paul uses action verbs, like patient and kind, to describe the virtues and attributes of love. Love is an entity beyond the understanding of mankind. It has no boundaries, barriers, or obstacles. It cannot be defined in human terms as best we would like too. Love as we know has existed for eons in our vast universe. God is both the author and the finisher of love. Love cannot be used as a weapon or an emotional tool to get our way. Paul illustrates this best when he writes that *"love is not boastful or proud or rude. It does not demand its own way. It is not irritable, and it keeps no record of being wronged."*

Love is not ours to give or take away. We cannot place conditions, standards, or even benchmarks on love. Yet every day, men and women do things they believe will win the affection or approval from someone or something. This false approval comes in many shapes and forms, from toxic relationships, verbal or physical abuse, drug, and alcohol intoxication, or even suicide from feeling rejected). To these people, love has become physical and not spiritual. Many of us only want to be loved and appreciated for who we are.

Millions have been hurt or cast aside and left to feel they can love no more. Even in the church, people have been hurt and rejected to the point that they no longer want to worship. We say that we love one another but hide behind such titles as elder, bishop, evangelist, and deacon as did the Pharisees and Sadducees. We demand people respect our titles instead of the Christ who we purport to live within us. How best should we exemplify the love of Christ in our everyday lives? In John 15:13, Christ tells us, *"Greater love hath no man than this, that a man lay down his life for his friends."* That means that our love for our fellow man must be action-oriented. It means getting down in that ditch with him or her when they are going through a crisis. I come to understand that one of the things the Bible is about is relationships. How can you have a relationship with God if you don't love those around you? *"For they loved human praise more than the praise of God"* (John 12:43). God did not put conditions on His love for us even in our sinful state. *"Yea, I have loved thee with an everlasting love: therefore with lovingkindness have I drawn thee"* (Jer. 31:3b).

The world that we now live in has not been kind. Billions have suffered and died because of a lack of love and compassion. Even Christ says, *"Your love for one another will prove to the world that you are my disciples"* (John 13:35). Thus, the question is how can we love those in the world who may not have a love for us? Christ was very specific in His commandant recorded in John 13:34: *"So now I am giving you a new commandment: Love each other. Just as I have loved you, you should love each other."* He is a living example of love. Following Him, no matter the circumstances or situation, we must love all, even those who detest us. We must humble and submit ourselves to Christ Jesus. Our walk with Him is one of meekness and self-denial. *"With all lowliness and meekness, with longsuffering, forbearing one another in love; Endeavouring to keep the unity of the Spirit in the bond of peace"* (Eph. 4:2-3). When Paul talks about, *"When I was a child, I spoke and thought and reasoned as a child. But when I grew up, I put away childish things"* in the eleventh verse of 1 Corinthians 13, he is extolling the spiritual maturity in our walk with Christ. There is no better illusion than that of coming to love God and our fellow man with all our hearts and minds.

> *And that ye put on the new man, which after God is created in righteousness and true holiness. Wherefore putting away lying, speak every man truth with his neighbour: for we are members one of another. Be ye angry, and sin not: let not the sun go down upon your wrath: Neither give place to the devil. Let him that stole steal no more: but rather let him labour, working with his hands the thing which is good, that he may have to give to him that needeth. Let no corrupt communication proceed out of your mouth, but that which is good to the use of edifying, that it may minister grace unto the hearers. And grieve not the Holy Spirit of God, whereby ye are sealed unto the day of redemption. Let all bitterness, and wrath, and anger, and clamour, and evil speaking, be put away from you, with all malice: And be ye kind one to another, tenderhearted, forgiving one another, even as God for Christ's sake hath forgiven you.* (Ephesians 4:24-32)

Even the disciple Stephen, who was stoned to death by a mad mob under the instruction of Paul who was then Saul in Acts 7:60 for daring to preach the pure unadulterated word of God, asks the Lord to have forgiveness on them. *"And he kneeled down, and cried out with a loud voice, Lord, lay not this sin to their charge. And when he had said this, he fell asleep"*

We must exemplify the love of Christ and our fellow man in our everyday dealings at work, in the gym, and at home. That means when someone does something that may be a transgression against us, we should not respond in anger but instead ask for God's wisdom in how to deal with that particular situation. *"Wherefore, my beloved brethren, let every man be swift to hear, slow to speak, slow to wrath"* (James 1:19). It is our spiritual maturity that we have developed and nurtured in God that enables the Holy Ghost to give us wisdom in how to deal with difficult situations. In all accounts, we must have love and empathy in our hearts.

If you are one who has sought love in all the wrong places, stop and take a look at what you are seeking and recognize that Jesus is the love that you desire and need. You must reflect and learn how to love yourself in the way that Jesus loves you. There is no need to speculate about what love is or how it feels, but rather accept and respond to Christ with a life that is a true sign of love. God has always loved us even when we did not always love Him. In Jeremiah 1:5 it says, *"He knew you before He formed you in your mother's womb."* God love's for us has always existed. How great is thy faithfulness? In Lamentations 3:22-23 it states, *"The faithful love of the Lord never ends! His mercies never cease. Great is his faithfulness, his mercies begin afresh each morning."* If you found yourself abandoned by your friends in your time of need then, in a toxic relationship, or mourning the loss of a loved one, then lay before the Cross and let Christ enter your life. Giving your life to Christ is the start of your healing process. The doors of the church are an open invitation of Christ who is embedded in you. Now all that is necessary is for you to come to Him.

Chapter 10

I Must Surrender

Humbleness, meekness, and submissions are the spiritual attributes in exercising a godly character in life and a personal relationship with Jesus Christ. God commands us to be humble not only when coming to Him, but also in our relationships with our family, co-workers, authority figures, and the stranger in the street. *"Better it is to be of a humble spirit with the lowly, than to divide the spoil with the proud"* (Prov. 16:19). To be truly humble in the eyesight of God is to deny one's self. *"Then said Jesus unto his disciples, If any man will come after me, let him deny himself, and take up his cross, and follow me"* (Matt. 16:24).

True denial of one's self is absolute submission and surrender to God recognizing the truth that it is He who is the guiding influence in our lives, not our personal beliefs and interests. In today's world, it has become increasingly difficult to live a chaste, humble, and victorious life for Jesus because some of us have allowed ourselves to be distracted from the will and presence of God in our life. We want to cater to self by indulging in the affairs of the world. *"And this I speak for your own profit; not that I may cast a snare upon you, but for that which is comely, and that ye may attend upon the Lord without distraction"* (1 Cor. 7:35). There is no doubt that in our folly of disobedience, we easily succumb vain things. We have let the world condition us to worship at the altar of the "want-it-now syndrome". We have become uncaring and self-centered in our destructive pursuit of gratuitous pleasure. *"The LORD knoweth the thoughts of man, that they are vanity"* (Prov. 94:11). Spiritual attributes, such as compassion, love, respect, empathy, and remorse, are looked upon with indifference. The world condemns these attributes as a sign of weakness and maintains gluttonous power is the physical avocation that one should seek.

There is no doubt that vanity is an infectious disease that has permeated the spiritual boundaries of the church. Parishioners, ministers, and all others in positions of spiritual authority have self-inflicted the church with a haughty spirit, wicked intend, and an evil mindset. The altar, pulpit, and pews have been polluted with the stench of wickedness. Instead of encouraging praying and helping our brothers and sisters, we have descended into a beasty debasement of character assassination, ostracizing, disrespect, and indifference to the plights that have besieged them. To say that God is displeased of what is happening in His house of worship is an understatement. *"Violence is risen up into a rod of wickedness: none of them shall remain, nor of their multitude, nor of any of theirs: neither shall there be wailing for them"* (Ezek. 7:11). Ultimate cruelty within the church and society has replaced Christ's gospel of love.

Today we are witnessing the last stages of a corrupt order that caters to the kingdom of Satan and not of God. Those of us who are still in the bosom of Christ must double-down and discipline our minds in our relationship with God by living a holy lifestyle. *"O worship the LORD in the beauty of holiness: fear before him, all the earth"* (Ps.96:9). That means advocating a life of denial both spiritually and naturally. Our focus should be on serving, obeying, and loving the Lord with all our heart and mind. We cannot allow ourselves to be caught up in the affairs and wickedness of the world. The self-destruction appetite of endless wars, economic disasters, violence, famine, disease, and starvation are as God has stated in His prophetic words through the preaching of His true prophets for a world that has turned its back on Him. *"And ye shall hear of wars and rumours of wars: see that ye be not troubled: for all these things must come to pass, but the end is not yet. For nation shall rise against nation, and kingdom against kingdom: and there shall be famines, and pestilences, and earthquakes, in divers places. All these are the beginning of sorrows"* (Matt. 24:6-8). It is a man who has brought the wrath of God upon him because he chooses to live for himself and not God.

When we live for God and not for ourselves through total submission; our actions are guided in a specific direction and a certain path. When God says go left, we go left. When He warns us not to go down a path, we obey. It is not for us to question, but to comply. *"For your obedience is come abroad unto all men. I am glad therefore on your behalf: but yet I would have you wise unto that which is good, and simple concerning evil"* (Rom. 16:19).

The spiritual characteristic of humility teaches us not only to love the Lord with all our hearts and mind, but also our friends, family, and enemies. Living a righteous life is a telling example that convicts the wicked and breaks the stronghold of Satan. This is because our walk with Christ is a mirror image of the trials and tribulations that He went through and His paying the ultimate price through His crucifixion so that we could have eternal life through Him without the burden of our sins. Humility strengthens our faith and resolves in Christ Jesus. From the onlooker's perspective, it may seem that being humble means weakness, yet they fail to see the inner man who strengthens because we are spiritually strong in Christ Jesus. *"And he said unto me, My grace is sufficient for thee: for my strength is made perfect in weakness. Most gladly therefore will I rather glory in my infirmities, that the power of Christ may rest upon me"* (2 Cor. 2:19).

Therefore, we should not be distraught through our trials, tribulations, and struggles in our lives and instead direct our energies in serving God no matter the circumstance. *"Though he slay me, yet will I trust in him: but I will maintain mine own ways before him"* (Job 13:15). Total submission to God means total victory because only He will deliver us from our affiliations. Victory is the reassurance that God who He says He is. *"He will swallow up death in victory; and the Lord GOD will wipe away tears from off all faces; and the rebuke of his people shall he take away from off all the earth: for the LORD hath spoken it"* (Isa. 25:18). When we let God govern our lives through humility, our journey through life becomes much more focused, meaningful, and blessed.

Therefore, why do we look for God in all the wrong places? We live in uncertain times that require maximum faith in our walk with God. These are times where Satan will try to take advantage of those of us who are not confident in our faith in God. We allow ourselves to become distracted and head down a different path He has not set. The end times we are now experiencing are no different than the sequence of events that besieged the people of Israel because of their spiritual and moral disobedience. In that period, the Jewish people became weak, disillusioned, and depressed because of the trials and tribulations afflicting them. Therefore, it became natural for them to latch on to any person who hung his shingles out and stated that they were a prophet of God. In Jeremiah 14:14-16, we find that God both warns us and educates us on the consequences of embracing those who were not sent by Him.

Then the LORD said unto me, The prophets prophesy lies in my name: I sent them not, neither have I commanded them, neither spake unto them: they prophesy unto you a false vision and divination, and a thing of nought, and the deceit of their heart". Therefore thus saith the LORD concerning the prophets that prophesy in my name, and I sent them not, yet they say, Sword and famine shall not be in this land; by sword and famine shall those prophets be consumed. And the people to whom they prophesy shall be cast out in the streets of Jerusalem because of the famine and the sword; and they shall have none to bury them, them, their wives, nor their sons, nor their daughters: for I will pour their wickedness upon them.

The people were deceived because they allowed their hearts and spirit man to be betrayed. They wanted to believe these prophets because they thought they represented the fastest path to get into God's will. In other words, they were looking for God in all the wrong places.

Today, we who are in the body of Christ have become a disobedient generation just as our forebears. We have fallen prey to the sweet words of unsound doctrine because we don't have the patience anymore to wait on God. In our zest and quest to accept the false teachings of false prophets as divine words from God, we have failed to adhere to the commandments Christ Jesus mandated in 2 Timothy 2:15: *"Study to shew thyself approved unto God, a workman that needeth not to be ashamed, rightly dividing the word of truth."* It is our responsibility as men and women of faith to not only investigate doctrine that is unsound but also to challenge the validity of the persons who dare to issue utterances of so-called biblical authority. *"All scripture is given by inspiration of God, and is profitable for doctrine, for reproof, for correction, for instruction in righteousness: That the man of God may be perfect, thoroughly furnished unto all good works"* (2 Tim. 3:16-17).

Therefore, what are the circumstances that would convince us to lower our spiritual armor of righteousness? The answer is quite obvious in that each one of us has gone through a crisis or trial that challenged our very walk with God and the belief in our abilities. These trials can come in the guise of health problems, financial ruin, job loss, infidelity, substance abuse, or the loss of a loved one among others. Sometimes these tribulations are constant and never seem to let up. All we have to do is look at all that Job went through; it serves as a constant reminder of our predicament. Some saints start to become weary with oppression because they don't believe that God will deliver them from their afflictions. They conclude either God does not hear their cries of anguish or that they have done something wrong to displease him. They become disillusioned and turn to the evil vices of soothsayers, new age prophets, or other types of medium to seek out God. They desire words that are soothing to their ears. As always, God warns us about lies ahead for those of us who seek a different path that does not edify Him. We once again turn to Timothy for an illustration of wickedness in high and low places.

> *This know also, that in the last days perilous times shall come. For men shall be lovers of their own selves, covetous, boasters, proud, blasphemers, disobedient to parents, unthankful, unholy, Without natural affection, trucebreakers, false accusers, incontinent, fierce, despisers of those that are good, Traitors, heady, highminded, lovers of pleasures more than lovers of God; Having a form of godliness, but denying the power thereof: from such turn away. For of this sort are*

they which creep into houses, and lead captive silly women laden with sins, led away with divers lusts, Ever learning, and never able to come to the knowledge of the truth. 2 Timothy 3:1-7.

We are looking for God in all the wrong places because we don't trust that God is who H says He is. We want God to respond to our needs on our time, not His. Our spiritual walk has become bogged down and corrupted in religious malfeasance. In our desire to draw nearer to God, we put ourselves out there by worshipping the god of this world, Satan, instead. *"And every spirit that confesseth not that Jesus Christ comes in the flesh is not of God: and this is that spirit of antichrist, whereof ye have heard that it should come; and even now already is it in the world"* (1 John 4:3).

We often place expectations on God that are naturally bound without spiritual roots. Some of us have decided to become pilgrims who will no longer pass through the gates of heaven but who have become a part of the world. *"No man can serve two masters: for either he will hate the one, and love the other; or else he will hold to the one, and despise the other. Ye cannot serve God and mammon"* (Matt. 6:24).

God wants all of us and not just parts of us. Just like any loving father would do, He demands obedience to His will and commandments. In serving God the Father, we cannot play fast and loose with our relationship with Him, putting ourselves out there in the world by exposing our spiritual temple to the polluted teachings of false prophets who have nothing but contempt for God and His Son, Jesus Christ. When our spiritual and natural temples are polluted, we cannot be fed the manna of knowledge from the Holy Spirit. Remember, our bodies do not belong to us but instead serve as a living testament to the awesome powers of God Almighty. *"What? know ye not that your body is the temple of the Holy Ghost which is in you, which ye have of God, and ye are not your own? For ye are bought with a price: therefore glorify God in your body, and in your spirit, which are God's."* (1 Cor. 6:19-20).

It is our responsibility to keep our spiritual and natural temple pure for the anointing of the Holy Spirit just as the Church, as the Bride of Christ, presents itself chaste and undefiled. It means fleeing from unsound doctrine and lifestyles that do not edify the Christ within us. That means living a holy lifestyle both in the natural and spiritual sense of the word. *"Having therefore these promises, dearly beloved, let us cleanse ourselves from all filthiness of the flesh and spirit, perfecting holiness in the fear of God"* (2 Cor. 7:1). If you are unsure of doctrine you don't consider sound, then it is up to you to seek wisdom and discernment from God Almighty. It also means strengthening yourself in the Word. *"In the beginning was the Word, and the Word was with God, and the Word was God"* (John 1:1).

A lot of us who reach an impasse fail to ask our fellow brothers and sisters for intercessory prayers to get us through on the other side. We may enter into our challenges and mess up, but we also can come out stronger on the other side if we would just let God do His will. This requires the total surrender of our life, trust, and hope to God. Some of us fail to give our problems to God because we want to fix things ourselves due to pride and arrogance on our part. It is that selfishness that prolongs our trial. Yet God has proven repeatedly that He is no respecter of man in His dealings with us.

Other times we cause troubles for ourselves by purposely being disobedient to God's will. God does send us warning signs about the wrong paths we have chosen. However, some of us choose to ignore the warnings and do what we want and when regardless of the consequences. It should come as no surprise then that God allows us to languish in our follies for a little awhile before delivering us from our afflictions. It is God's imperative to decide when, how, and where He will deliver us from our ordeal. This is all to teach us that He is indeed God all by Himself.

The best place to seek God during your time of greatest need is in a quiet place. That can be in your office, home, hotel room, a rowboat, or even deep-sea diving. Any place is alright to seek God because it is just you and Him there. His last days on earth before His crucifixion, Christ sought out the confines of Gethsemane to have His quiet time with God. *"Then cometh Jesus with them unto a place called Gethsemane, and saith unto the disciples, Sit ye here, while I go and pray yonder"* (Matt. 26:36).

The other place to seek out God is your place of worship with your pastor and fellow church members. You can form a prayer chain of intercessory prayer that can be a 24/7 vigil until there is a breakthrough. However, be forewarned that we must come to God with genuine humility and need or He will not answer those prayers. Brothers and sisters do not mock God with your superfluous words.

> *And when thou prayest, thou shalt not be as the hypocrites are: for they love to pray standing in the synagogues and in the corners of the streets, that they may be seen of men. Verily I say unto you, They have their reward. But thou, when thou prayest, enter into thy closet, and when thou hast shut thy door, pray to thy Father which is in secret; and thy Father which seeth in secret shall reward thee openly. But when ye pray, use not vain repetitions, as the heathen do: for they think that they shall be heard for their much speaking.*
> Matthew 6: 5-7

Being with like-minded brothers and sisters will serve as another layer of spiritual armour for protection against the supernatural bombardments by Satan and his cast of cohorts. When we stray outside the fold of God's love and commandments by being lured by some quick fix soothsayers, it makes us vulnerable and easy prey to the temptation of the flesh and spirit. We don't need to seek God in the wrong places because He has been here with us all the time. *"What shall we then say to these things? If God be for us, who can be against us?"* (Rom. 8:31). Also, in seeking God, the Bible clearly instructs us to crucify our flesh daily so we can be pure of heart and spirit in our walk with Christ Jesus. *"And they that are Christ's have crucified the flesh with the affections and lusts"* (Gal. 5:24).

When we get right with God there is nothing he will not do for any of us. He already knows the desires of our hearts before we come to Him in prayer. *"For I know the thoughts that I think toward you, saith the LORD, thoughts of peace, and not of evil, to give you an expected end"* (Jer. 29:11). No matter what the circumstances or the ordeal, we must trust God and not try to second guess His intentions or plans. *"Trust in the LORD with all thine heart, and lean not unto thine own understanding. In all thy ways acknowledge him, and he shall direct thy paths"* (Prov. 3:5-6). My brothers and sisters, every place that God has dominion is the right place to seek Him. In essence, the only right place to seek God is in His bosom of protection and unconditional love.

Irrelevant Truths

The question always asked is what is the truth? It is a question that has been pondered, analyzed, and examined by so-call experts for thousands of years. Many organizations, governments, religious orders, and individuals have all laid claim to what the truth is. What is abnormal has been proclaimed normal and that which is normal has been cursed as abnormal. In essence, the world has become more deeply confused in the complex webs of lies, distortions, conspiracies, and half-truths. It's no wonder that John the Baptist stayed out in the wilderness eating locust and wearing animal skin. The elite of that time considered him a wild man of bestial nature. Could it be the elites who passed false judgment on him were themselves, wild men, with bestial intentions who covered them up with a facade of fashionable civility?

Is it possible that what they passed off as civilization was nothing more than anarchy to John the Baptist? He had the hindsight to see through the phony airs and hypocrisy of the so-called educated men at that time. Their education was one of ignorance, pride, and selfishness. They expected the world to cater to them and not them to the world. In the end, they killed a peaceful man from Galilee who dared to bring forth a gospel of truth, love, forgiveness, and mutual understanding.

Strangely enough, we find ourselves in the same type of situation in direct comparison to John the Baptist. We have an entrenched elite that tries to define truth to us in a confusing maze of print, the internet and television media, and government and corporate propaganda. All this misdirects, confuses, divides, and dilutes what is true. These elite have turned man against his kind in a bestial type of way. We view each other around the world with contempt, suspicion, hatred, and animosity. We have killed and continue to kill in the name of false doctrine that we consider the truth but have no understanding ourselves. We have built imaginary walls to separate us from one another spiritually and psychologically. We don't believe that God made man in His image. We tend to think that He made some men in His image; the rest we consider heathens outside of His majesty. We have made a false truth a graven image unto ourselves. We have become demigods of arrogance, lust, and selfishness. We have glorified the powerful at the expense of the needy and chastised the weak for not being strong like the morally corrupt.

Therefore, I would like to speak against this. First, I believe Jesus is indeed coming back, but not in the way we expect Him. *Behold, he cometh with clouds; and every eye shall see him, and they [also] which pierced him: and all kindreds of the earth shall wail because of him. Even so, Amen.* (Revelation 1:7 KJV). Jesus is waiting on His children to grow up and finally realize we are all His creation regardless of race, creed, religion, sex, or nationality. He is expecting the few of us who get it to lead the rest of us to that truthful understanding. He expects us to love one another in an intimate, nourishing, and caring way. He expects us to better ourselves technologically, economically, and culturally by eliminating poverty, disease, hunger, homelessness, and violence against the oppressed. He expects us as Scripture portrays to establish schools, clean up the environment, house those without shelter, and give jobs to all who desire work. He wants us to use our minds to explore the universe, make scientific discoveries, compose beautiful songs, create wonderful paintings, and write Nobel Prize-winning literature. God wants us to truly examine the inner souls of our being to experience true love, respect, and humility toward one another. You see, God is the essence of true love because it has no boundaries and cannot be defined or typecast. Love is above all reproach whether it is physical, material, or mental. Love is not oppression; it is the liberation of the soul, mind, and body. It transcends a physical bond, such as sex, and manifests itself int a spiritual path of enlightenment.

That is real truth in its entirety. It goes beyond the avenues of normal and abnormal. What is needed is for humanity to cease its path of self-destruction and start acting like the creation God intended us to be.

Chapter 11

A Physical Only Abstinence Mindset

Over the past decade, organizations, such as religious institutions and the federal government, have spent a great deal of time, money, and energy to stem the tide of rising promiscuity, drug use, gang activities, and crime within our Black community. Everyone from athletes, military personnel, executives, teachers, social workers, clergy, and entertainment have extolled the virtues of abstinence from these terrible things. A big emphasis has been placed on the physical aspect of abstinence as a final process. The practice of abstinence as a physical process is defined as "the act or practice of refraining from indulging an appetite or desire, especially for alcoholic drink or sexual intercourse" (The Free Dictionary 2020).

Unfortunately, the physical emphasis of abstinence as a tool to stop increased promiscuity in all its forms is seriously flawed because it has no biblical or spiritual foundation. Therefore, it is no wonder that the success rates of abstinence-only programs in this country are dismal at best. The Bible is very specific about the emphasis on the spirit of man in the glorification and edification of God. *"And the very God of peace sanctify you wholly,* and I pray God your whole spirit and soul and body be preserved blameless unto the coming of our Lord Jesus Christ" (1 Thess. 5:23). We, as children of the Most High God, must present our body to Him blameless and faultless because it does not belong to us. The body is a temple for the indwelling of the Holy Spirit. *"What? Know ye not that your body is the temple of the Holy Ghost which is in you, which ye have of God, and ye are not your own?" (1 Cor. 6:19.)* The process of cleansing ourselves and making our bodies presentable to God is both spiritual and natural. In the Old Testament, priests had to go through a cleansing process before offering a sacrifice to God Almighty for the atonement of sins and forgiveness. *"When thou hast made an end of cleansing it, thou shalt offer a young bullock without blemish, and a ram out of the flock without blemish" (Ezek. 43:23).*

The presence of Christ on earth as God manifested in the flesh changed all of that because He was the worthy example of perfection both naturally and spiritually. *"Think not that I am come to destroy the law, or the prophets: I am not come to destroy, but to fulfill" (Matt. 5:17).* It was Christ who gave life to the law by making it a living organism. Christ expected us to follow Him and not the avenues of the world. *"For what shall it profit a man, if he shall gain the whole world, and lose his own soul?" (Mark 8:36).* His death on the cross and physical resurrection freed us from the bondage of trying to obey all the laws from a physical process. Even Christ's death and resurrection were physical; living our life through Him is spiritual. In other words, we became a new creature through the blood of Jesus Christ who served as the ultimate sacrifice for the atonement of our sins and shortcomings. *"Therefore if any man be in Christ, he is a new creature: old things are passed away; behold, all things are become new" (2 Cor. 5:17).*

Thus, the physical act of abstinence is useless unless we have a spiritual mindset focused on Christ Jesus. *"Dearly beloved, I beseech you as strangers and pilgrims, abstain from fleshly lusts, which war against the soul" (1 Peter 2:11).* True abstinence means crucifying the flesh daily, both naturally and spiritually. *"And they that are Christ's have crucified the flesh with the affections and lusts" (Gal. 5:24).* It is the temptation of the flesh that separates us from the perfect will of God. *"Harden not your hearts, as in the provocation, in the day of temptation in the wilderness" (Heb. 3:8).* To resist the temptation of the flesh, one must have an understanding of what the attributes of iniquity are. The Bible is very specific in identifying the iniquities of the flesh. *"For all that is in the world, the lust of the flesh, and the lust of the eyes, and the pride of life, is not of the Father, but is of the world" (1 John 2:16).*

True abstinence is not only a spiritual and natural approach; it also includes having the right mindset. One should abstain from sin because one wants to be in the perfect will of the Father. That means having a victorious mindset from sin by setting oneself apart (sanctified) from the world. It means living a holy lifestyle in body, mind, and spirit. Holiness implies having an incorruptible nature that is not susceptible to the desires of the flesh. *"To the end he may stablish your hearts unblameable in holiness before God, even our Father, at the coming of our Lord Jesus Christ with all his saints" (1 Thess. 3:13).* If we teach our young people the ways of holiness by living a victorious life through Christ Jesus, they will have not only the biblical but moral foundation to be successful in abstaining from the vices of the world.

This flesh or beast that lurks behind church work as a means of salvation stands within the doors of the fellowship hall, promoting mischief, lying, and manipulating situations for allegiance and authority from private interpretations and family exaltations. *"But there was a certain man, called Simon, which beforetime in the same city used sorcery, and bewitched the people of Samaria, giving out that himself was some great one: To whom they all gave heed, from the least to the greatest, saying, This man is the great power of God" (Acts 8:9-10).*

This beast (your flesh) raises its ugly head in the morning, props itself in the noonday, and struts its stuff during the night. There is no special time it appears; it is there consistently and, constantly any moment of the day. It speaks when it should not, it acts when it is provoked, it kills, and it destroys. Calamity is its foreplay, destruction is its desire, and death is its destination.

The beast of your flesh hides behind degrees of education, false senses of reality, and the allusion of self-importance. The flesh continues triumvirate its worth (arrogance), value (pride), and placement (pompous circumstance), distributing its thoughts of importance, trying to inset its way into the lives, places, and things of people. *"And when Simon saw that through laying on of the apostles' hands the Holy Ghost was given, he offered them money, Saying, Give me also this power, that on whomsoever I lay hands, he may receive the Holy Ghost. But Peter said unto him, Thy money perish with thee, because thou has thought that the gift of God may be purchased with money. Thou hast neither part nor lot in this matter: for thy heart is not right in the sight of God" (Acts 8:18-21).*

How many people do you see in the household of faith who construct their walk as Simon? Simon's flesh wanted recognition and power, and that is the sinful nature that we must be delivered from. Our flesh continues to seek validation from anyone who will listen or be a party to at any cost. Our flesh comes in all shapes, form, and color, yet it is unrecognizable to the naked eye because it is hidden within your members— your attitude, thoughts, action, and deeds— and only time will cause it to show its many ugly faces.

Let's look at this more closely. What do you think is the mindset of Simon? and Peter's response to Simon. Acts 8:18-19 When Simon saw that the Spirit was given at the laying on of the apostles' hands, he offered them money and said, "Give me also this ability so that everyone on whom I lay my hands may receive the Holy Spirit." Now, let's look at Peter's response to Simon. Peter answered: "May your money perish with you because you thought you could buy the gift of God with money! You have no part or share in this ministry because your heart is not right before God. (verse 20-21).

Repent—this is the first step in conversion. Simon was not directed to pray first. His first indispensable work was to repent, that is, to exercise proper sorrow for his sin and to abandon his plans. This shows first, that all sinners are exhorted to repent as their first work. They are not told to wait, and read, and pray in the expectation that repentance will be given them. Secondly, prayer will not be accepted or heard unless the sinner regrets his sin and desires to be forsaken. Then, and then only, will he be heard. When he comes loving his sins, resolving to still practice them, God will not hear him. When he comes desirous of forsaking them, grieved that he is guilty, and feeling his need for help, God will hear his prayer.

"Therefore of this thy wickedness," the passage says. This clarifies Simon's incorrect act. His offer shows a state of mind altogether inconsistent with true religion—that which was his character. Next comes, *"and pray God"* which should be with a desire, purpose, and state of mind to forsake sin which opens God to hear the prayer.

Sinners are directed to repent their conduct, not because they have the promise of forgiveness, and not because they hope to be forgiven, but because sin is a great evil, and it is right and proper that they should repent, whether they are forgiven or not. That is to be left to the sovereign mercy of God. The sullied are to repent of sin; they are to feel they have any claim on God, but that they are dependent on Him and must be saved or lost at His will. Their tears are not what purchase forgiveness, but their action of laying at God's foot of mercy hoping through faith that God will forgive. *"The thought* [the secret purpose of the soul] *of thine heart may be forgiven thee" (Acts 8:22).*

"For I perceive that thou art in the gall of bitterness and in the bond of iniquity" (Acts 8:23). Some would say at this moment Peter was judging the heart, however, Peter judged, as all other men would, by the act. The heart of Simon was full of malignant sin that ruled over him and bound him as a slave just as it does to you and me today. *"Thy way and thy doings have procured these things unto thee; this is thy wickedness, because it is bitter, because it reacheth unto thine heart" (Jer. 4:18).*

Let us look deeper. Romans 7:17, 20-22 states:

> *Now then it is no more I that do it, but sin that dwelleth in me, For I know that in me (that is, in my flesh,) dwelleth no good thing: for to will is present with me; but how to perform that which is good I find not, that I do... For the good that I would I do not: but the evil which I would not, that I do. Now if I do that I would not, it is no more I that do it, but sin that dwelleth in me. I find then a law, that, when I would do good, evil is present with me: For I delight in the law of God after the inward man.*

Note: the inward man is Christ Jesus the hope of glory.

Paul's statement *"Now then it is no more I that do it, but sin that dwelleth in me"* should not be taken as a renunciation of his responsibility for his actions, but rather as his revealing the nature of the inner conflict between his two natures. Paul was giving us a personal example of who he was struggling with his flesh.

1) To will (the first nature), which is his attitude;

2) To perform (the second nature, which is to accomplish that what is good that Paul could not do).

"But I see another law in my members, warring against the law of my mind, and bringing me into captivity to the law of sin which is in my members:" (Rom. 2:23). Here Paul continues to speak of the good he desired to do but did not do. And the sin (missing the mark) that he continued to do. He is showing a war between the flesh and the spirit man. The flesh doesn't want to do what is right. The spirit walks within the authority and power of God. Here you see conflicts.

However, it is not over yet; there is a way to overcome it. In his realization of his sinful nature, Paul cries out, *"O wretched man that I am! Who shall deliver me from the body of this death"* *(Acts 7: 24).* After asking for repentance and coming to the understanding that he is wretched—there was nothing the flesh could do to help him, nothing the flesh could do to pay for this death, nothing the flesh could give for the deliverance from the body of sin—he finally breaks down and says, *"I thank God through Jesus Christ our Lord. So then with the mind (understanding, attitude), I myself serve the law of God; but with the flesh the law of sin"* (Acts 7:25).

Therefore, the only avenue, the only route to save us from this beast that continues to transform itself. is Christ! Oh, bless His name! For Scripture states with this freedom, with this deliverance, with this hope, with this survival, *"For the law of the Spirit of life in Christ Jesus hath made me free from the law of sin and death. For what the law* (moral law – The Ten Commandments & more) *could not do in that it was weak through the flesh, God sending his own Son in the likeness of sinful flesh, and for sin, condemned sin in the flesh: That the righteousness of the law might be fulfilled in us, who walk not after the flesh, but after the Spirit" (Rom. 8: 2-4).* God has given us to be overcomers through Him.

Now, let's look at flesh as a verb. I will attempt to attack several areas of the flesh and make directions to its other infractions.

In defining the flesh of action as a verb, the 1828 version of the Merriam-Webster Dictionary offers the second definition "To harden; to accustom; to establish in any practice." (Merriam-Webster 1828). Imagine men fleshed in cruelty, women fleshed in malice. Scripture states it as, this: *now the works* (action) *of the flesh are manifest* (see openly), *which are these; adultery, fornication, uncleanness, lasciviousness, idolatry, witchcraft, hatred, variance, emulations, wrath, strife, seditions, heresies, envying's, murders, drunkenness, revellings, and such like: of the which I tell you before, as I have also told you in time past, that they which do such things shall not inherit the kingdom of God" (Gal. 5:19-21 KJV).

A comparable scriptural text is found in Romans 1:22-32. *"Professing themselves to be wise, they became fools, And changed the glory of the uncorruptible God into an image made like to corruptible man, and to birds, and four-footed beast, and creeping things. Wherefore God also gave them up to uncleanness through the lusts of their own hearts, to dishonour their own bodies between themselves."*

How is this consistent with God's holiness and hatred of sin? God neither indoctrinates sin into their hearts, nor excites sinning in their lives, but leaves sinners to themselves to act without restraining according to the inclination of their lusts and corruptions. Also, it gives them up to Satan, that unclean spirit who never fails to provoke the unrepentant to uncleanness as he knows their lust stands ready to comply with every act. As to their idolatry, Paul tells us at the twenty-third verse that people that change the uncorruptible God into a corruptible beast had made false and unworthy representations of the ever-blessed God.

Can you not see this happening in the religious world today? Men and women purport to know the Bible front to back, yet they are not living a single verse though they try to dictate how you should live. They flaunt their sin of lust and strut their lies of deceit across the pulpit. The Bible describes people like these as, *"Ever learning, and never able to come to the knowledge of the truth" (2 Tim.3:7)*.

As to their uncleanness, Paul shows that they were so given up to the lust for sinning against the light of nature, they forsook the order of nature and were more brutish than the very brutes. *"Who changed the truth of God into a lie and worshipped and served the creature more than the Creator, who is blessed forever. Amen"* (Rom. 7:25). In this verse, they are charged with a false object of their worship, giving divine honor to a creature. They changed the truth of God into a lie; a false idol which is the same a lie because it deceives men by seeming to be what it is not; it seems in the idolater's fancy to have some divinity in it when, in reality, it is but wood or stone. Every image of God is a false and lying representation of God.

Let's look at another scripture. Genesis 3:1-6 shows the false and lying representation of God in the form of the serpent. *"Now the serpent was more subtle."*

Webster's defines subtle as: 1) Sly; artful; cunning; crafty; insinuating; as a subtle person; a subtle adversary. 2) Planned by art; deceitful; as a subtle scheme. 3) Deceitful; treacherous than any beast of the field. You can see all of this in Eve's interactions with the snake (Merriam-Webster 2020)

> *And he said unto the woman, Yea, hath God said, Ye shall not eat of every tree of the garden? And the woman said unto the serpent, We may eat of the fruit of the trees of the garden: But of the fruit of the tree which is in the midst of the garden, God hath said, we shall not eat of it, neither shall ye touch it, lest ye die. And the serpent said unto the woman, Ye shall not surely die: For God doth know that in the day ye eat thereof, then your eyes shall be opened, and ye shall be as gods, knowing good and evil.*

God has given a commandment and has set a boundary line between obedience and disobedience.

Obedience = Physical and Spiritual Life (Genesis 3:3)

Disobedience = Physical and Spiritual Death (Genesis 3:6).

The devil took a little of God's word and took a whole lot of himself to sway Eve. Adam and Eve knew what was good for they were holy in all points. So, all that they could learn from being disobedient is sin; *For God doth know that in the day ye eat thereof, then your eyes shall be opened, and ye shall be as gods, knowing good and evil.* (Gen 3:5). Here is deception in its fullest as Scripture states: "*But every man is tempted, when he is drawn away of his own lust, and enticed*" (James 1:14).

> "*And when the woman saw that the tree was good for food* (<u>lust of the flesh</u>) *and that it was pleasant to the*

eyes (<u>lust of the eyes</u>), and a tree to be desired to make one wise (<u>pride of life</u>), she took of the fruit thereof, and did eat, and gave also unto her husband with her; and he did eat" (Gen 3:6).

"For all that is in the world, the lust of the flesh and the lust of the eyes, and the pride of life, is not of the Father, but is of the world" (1 John 2:16)

Learn hence that when men provoke God to forsake them and judicially give them up to their own, they will commit such monstrous and unnatural uncleanness being the very brutes they are. Within this, they find others who seek out such things as they do. The age-old adage "birds of a feather flock together" readily applies to men who sin together.

For this cause God gave them up unto vile affections: for even their women did change the natural use into that which is against nature: And likewise also the men, leaving the natural use of the woman, burned in their lust one toward another; men with men working that which is unseemly, and receiving in themselves that recompence of their error which was meet. And even as they did not like to retain God in their knowledge, God gave them over to a reprobate mind, to do those things which are not convenient; Being filled with all unrighteousness, fornication, wickedness, covetousness, maliciousness; full of envy, murder, debate, deceit, malignity; whisperers, Backbiters, haters of God, despiteful, proud, boasters, inventors of evil things, disobedient to parents, Without understanding, covenant breakers, without natural affection, implacable, unmerciful: Who knowing the judgment of God, that they which commit such things are worthy of death, not only do the same, but have pleasure in them that do them. Romans 1:26-32

Scripture is self-explanatory and gives credence to the flesh and its nature. It relates to reprobate men and women burning in their beastly lusts towards those of the same sex. First, they were haters of God, not of His essence, being, and goodness, and then they were haters of His holiness, justice, and providence. Secondly, they were without natural affection: men with men, women with women, fathers with daughters and mothers with sons, given over to pedophilia, adultery, bestiality, orgies, etc. Finally, despising and hating one another, as soon as they fell out with God (not retaining who He is) they fell out with themselves. They knew their unnatural lusts deserved death and the wrath of God, but that did not prevent their behaviors. Not only did they personally commit these sins, but they also took pleasure and delight in those who committed them. This was the height of their wickedness. It is greater wickedness to approve and applaud sin than acting and delighting in it within yourselves. As it is written in the Bible, *"For he that soweth to his flesh shall of the flesh reap corruption; but he that soweth to the Spirit shall of the Spirit reap life everlasting"* (Gal. 6:8).

Finally, let's look at another figure in the Word of God. Thomas (some call him Doubting Thomas) needed to settle in his mind whether it was Christ or not. He needed to touch the very place where the nails had severed the flesh from the bones to believe. Was it the doubting of Christ's existence and power or his self-awareness? Then afterward found himself in the eyes of Christ What a revelation of God's power in us as the hope of glory! So, Thomas bowed humbly and submissively to the will of God who then sent him unto a dying nation, one that sought their own beliefs, glorification, and satisfaction. Yes, since that time, this perverse generation continues to be trapped in a world of self-worship, self-confidence, and self-congratulation.

Chapter 12

Manifestations of an Evil Nature

Pantheist belief holds that not only is man good, but man is also god. We just need to recognize the fact, it continues. However, like naturalism, pantheism doesn't allow for a personal God inside or outside the physical universe.

Traditional pantheism sees God as an infinite, impersonal force that encompasses all of reality. All is one, all is god. Americanized pantheism, or the New Age Movement, adds an evolutionary element. It sees men and women becoming one with the universal mind as a continuation of material evolution through the animal kingdom.

Unlike naturalism, pantheism sees man's problem as a spiritual one. It marks that, somehow, mankind has collectively forgotten its oneness with the universe. This separates man from understanding the true nature of things and, according to New Age teaching, visits upon him all the suffering of our current world and leaves him without the power to make reality conform to his bidding. So, man is good. We've just forgotten our oneness. The solution is education. We need to be enlightened. We need to have our spiritual eyes opened so we can visualize world peace.

Naturalism States:

1. Man is the product of his environment.

    As the product of evolution, man is just a more highly evolved animal. He is the product of his environment. This is the underlying assumption of behavioral psychologists like Pavlov, Maslow, and Skinner. When it comes to the nature of man, they were the most consistent naturalists. Skinner said that the mind was a myth—that thoughts were simply chemical processes responding to physical stimuli. Men simply respond to their environment. As such, man does not have free will. Therefore, if you find yourself committing a crime, it's not your fault. It's because of the way you were raised or because of your present circumstances. Therefore, you shouldn't be punished. For example, some school children once defaced or destroyed some school property. The teacher being interviewed said, "They are good kids, but they… come from under-privileged homes." That statement reveals what that teacher's view of human nature is. Man is good, but society makes them do bad things. There are a couple of logical problems with this view. Would it not also be true, that if you dive in front of a car to save someone, it's not your fault either. So, you wouldn't want to accept any praise or reward for saving that person.

    Very few naturalists are intellectually honest and consistent with their world view when it comes to human nature. They pick and choose what they want and borrow from the Christian world view. They want to take credit for their good deeds, and they want to believe that they are in control of their own destiny. But they are quick to say that man is good, and things like poverty, ignorance, abuse, etc. make him do bad things. If this is true, then creating the perfect society will end crime and abuse, etc.

Another big problem with this view is this: If a man is basically good, how did we get a bad society to start with? It would seem the first society would have been made by good people, been perfect from the start, and stayed perfect. There is a logical problem with this, but that doesn't deter anyone.

Marxism, Communism, and Socialism are prime examples of the naturalist world view. Evil is defined as capitalism where the wealthy oppress the poor. If everyone in society is equal, then everyone will choose to act properly. Individuals will work to the best of their ability and take only what they need from the community. So, naturalism relieves man of guilt. He is just the product of his environment.

2. There is a tendency toward improvement.

Naturalism and evolution teach us that there is in nature an inherent tendency towards improvement. People don't just apply this principle to the physical world. Things tend to fall apart without an external force maintaining it. In the moral and spiritual realm, that external force (really an internal force) is the Holy Spirit. Despite what the rationalists say, you can't just teach morality and expect men to follow the rules. People don't usually do what they know is right. They do what they love to do. They do what makes them feel good, which gives them power, prestige, and more. Education doesn't make people good. It just makes smarter sinners. Anyone who studies history knows that nations may start good and grow for a while, but then immorality sets in; everyone does what is right in their own eyes and society fails.

We see it repeatedly in the Bible. For example, look especially in the book of Judges. The book of Judges covers a chaotic period in Israel's history between the years 1380 and 1050 B.C. Israel continually did evil before the eyes of the Lord. God delivered them into the hands of various oppressors. Each time the people cried out to the Lord, He faithfully raised a judge who brought deliverance to His people. The book of Judges recounts the sad events of Israel's apostasy. It was common in Israel during this period for every man to do *"that which was right in his own eyes"* (Judg. 17:6; 21:25). By breaking this book down, we find it is divided into three principal sections: Prologue (introduction: chapters 1 and 2); Main body (narrative accounts of the judges who led the people (chapters 3 through 16); and an Epilogue (a conclusion which describes the social and spiritual state of the people (chapters 17 through 21). The first part of the prologue presents the historical stage where the stories that follow are developed. It describes the incomplete conquest of the Promised Land and the Lord's punishment for Israel's unfaithfulness to the Covenant. The second part presents Israel's rebellions in the first centuries of its life in the Promised Land and shows how God dealt with His people during that period, an era characterized by a recurrent cycle of apostasy, oppression, repentance, and deliverance.

Even as we move towards the first part of the gospel, we still find that man is a sinner and needs a savior. In short, if you take away the gospel, then you don't have God's people being saved. Jesus becomes just an example to follow. You don't have the Holy Spirit indwelling, leading, and guiding people to all truth, taking on the personification of Jesus Christ and becoming His followers. Then there is no fruit of the Spirit because there is no Spirit. Those who fail to do this are selfish, and they do what is good for themselves—just as the days of old.

In this realm of thought, you find also altruistic people who believe, since we are created in the image of God, we can do good. Being deprived doesn't mean we are always as bad as we can be. Altruism was coined by Auguste Comte, the French founder of positivism, to describe the ethical doctrine he supported. He believed individuals had a moral obligation to serve the interest of others or the "greater good" of humanity. However, Nietzsche supported egoism and pointed out that such a position is degrading and demeaning to the individual (Leiter 2020).

People with a non-Christian world view often borrow from Christianity and try to be moral without the proper foundation (i.e., *"As it was in the days of Noah, so shall it be also in the days of the Son of man."*(Matt. 24:37). Then, the world was destroyed by a flood; in our day, it is to be destroyed by fire. The message of warning is going forth to the world to prepare a people who will be saved out of the general ruin of earthly things. We are living in a very solemn time, and solemn thoughts should occupy the mind; the earnest inquiry should be made by every soul, *"What shall I do to be saved?"* (Acts 16:30).

The message that the coming of Jesus Christ is at hand is not received. The thought that He is at the door is not welcome. Just as the message of the coming deluge was rejected in the time of Noah, so the announcement of the final destruction of this world is disbelieved and mocked. Thousands will reason in the same manner as ancient people in the days before the flood. The message of truth was refused and people turned away to their businesses, farms, relationships and the pleasures of life Look what is said in Luke 14:20. They responded to the invitation of Jesus to come, for the feast was now ready, *"I have married a wife, and therefore I cannot come."* Jesus the Christ declared, *"For us it was in the days that were before the flood, they were eating, and drinking, marrying and giving in marriage, until the day that Noah entered into the ark, and knew not until the flood came, and took them all away; so shall also the coming of the Son of man be"* (Matt. 24:38-39). He foresaw that men would be engaged in every selfish work, living without fear of God, when the day of final judgment was near.

> *This know also, that in the last days perilous times shall come. For men shall be lovers of their own selves, covetous, boasters, proud, blasphemers, disobedient to parents, unthankful, unholy, without natural affection, trucebreakers, false-accusers, incontinent, fierce, despisers of those that are good, traitors, heady, highminded, lovers of pleasures more than lovers of Yahuwah.* 2 Timothy 3:1-3

And while they are crying, *For when they shall say, Peace and safety; then sudden destruction cometh upon them, as travail upon a woman with child; and they shall not escape.* (1Thess. 5:3 KJV).

In the days of Noah, the earth was filled with violence. Is it not in a similar condition today? Of the vast population in the world before the flood, only eight persons were saved from destruction. The mass of mankind than would not listen to the warning of the servant of the Master. In our own day, the majority of men will *"turn away their ears from hearing the truth and shall be turned unto fables"* (2 Tim. 4:4). People in Noah's age were intensely worldly, full of hatred, malice, self-deceit, and greed. They were without the fear of God; God was not in all their thoughts. They had no care whether He approved their course or not. They were eating and drinking, marrying, and giving in marriage with no thought of their Creator or their responsibility to Him. The people indulged their appetites and the baser passions (wants of the body: hunger, lust, fear, etc., as opposed to the wants of the mind or the soul: beauty, justice, love) until they were and abhorrence in the sight of the Holy God. They became the slaves of that which was vile, and they made a god of this world.

The great crime in the marriages of the days of Noah was that the sons of God formed alliances with the daughters of men. It was a joining of those who professed to acknowledge and revere

God with those who were corrupt of heart. Without discrimination, they married whom they would. Many in this day who have no depth of religious experience will do the same things as were done in the days of Noah. They will enter marriage without careful and prayerful consideration. The thought of marriage seems to have a bewitching power. You know the ritual: two persons become acquainted, then infatuated with each other, and their whole attention is absorbed. The reason is blinded, and judgment is overthrown. They will not submit to any advice or control, but insist on having their way, regardless of consequences. Like a contagion, that must run its course, there seems to be no such thing as putting a stop to it. If they were going to church, they lose interest in prayer meetings and everything that pertains to religion. They are wholly infatuated with each other, and neglect the duties of life as something of little concern. Night after night, they burn the midnight oil to talk with each other about frivolous subjects of no importance. Their hearts speak lies, profanity, and lust.

> *Wherefore gird up the loins of your mind, be sober, and hope to the end for the grace that is to be brought unto you at the revelation of Jesus Christ; As obedient children, not fashioning yourselves according to the former lusts in your ignorance: But as he which hath called you is holy, so be ye holy in all manner of conversation.* 1 Peter 1:13-15 KJV.

If only they could have their eyes opened, they would see an angel making a record of their words and acts violating the laws of health and modesty. These hours of midnight dissipation frequently lead to the ruin of both parties. Satan is exalted, and God is dishonored when men and women dishonor themselves by the spell of this infatuation.

The marriage of such persons cannot be solemnized under the approval of God because they are married. After all, passion (lust) moved them. When the novelty of the affair is over, they will begin to realize what they have done. In six months after the vows are spoken, they will see their sentiments toward each other have become strained and sometimes volatile. The love is gone. Each discovers the other's imperfections that laid masked under the deception of infatuation. The promises at the altar do not bind them together. In consequence of hasty marriages, even among the professed people of God, there are separations, divorces, and great confusion in the church. This kind of marrying and giving in marriage is one of Satan's special devices to deceive the very biblical principle of Jesus' marriage to the bride.

Chapter 13

How Can I Escape?

You ask, then, how can you escape? How do you get rid of something that continues to be at the forefront of your life? Although Genesis 1:26 says God created man in His image, this does not mean physical likeness. God is Spirit. Although the Bible speaks of the "hand" of God, it also speaks of being "sheltered under His wing." These are just word pictures to help us understand concepts about God. Being in the image of God refers to our personality, intelligence, conscience, and awareness of right and wrong. We are individual and moral creatures. Because we are in the image of God, we are capable of loving, doing good deeds, and sacrificing.

So, our creation explains why we are capable of great good. We've seen what the three major world views say about man's basic nature as it relates to being good or bad. But let's look at another aspect of the nature of man. Man is unique from animals is his ability to think logically. Although an animal might learn how to navigate a maze and do so faster and faster each time, animals don't engage in abstract thinking. They don't form different types of governments. They don't develop advanced technology. A beaver house looks the same now as it has for thousands of years. A bird's nest looks the same now as it always has. If a man is just a more highly evolved animal, how does naturalism explain this huge leap in intelligence? But if we were created in the image of God, then man's vast difference from the animals makes sense.

According to Genesis 2:8, 16-17, God put Adam and Eve in a perfect environment with everything they needed. (Remember, naturalism says if we just had a perfect environment, everyone would be good.) He gave them a command to obey. God didn't want robots. He wanted creatures who chose to have fellowship with Him.

Man disobeyed, as recorded in Genesis 3:1-24. We see their guilt, and how (the world was affected). The result was immediate spiritual death and eventual physical death. Because of the fall, the image of God was corrupted. And the Bible teaches that Adam's sin was passed on to the whole human race. Romans 5:12 says, *"So then, just as sin entered the world through one man and death through sin, and so death spread to all people because all sinned."* In Psalm 51:5, David says, *"Look, I was prone to do wrong from birth; I was a sinner the moment my mother conceived me."*

So, the fall also explains why man is capable of great evil. Satan has his agenda, and this agenda continues to move towards a war of perpetual destruction and death against the soul. It solicits the lust of the world and its seductive desires as its. It incorporates its mind of deceit, lust, and covetousness. It isn't bothered perpetuating its lies to get what it wants. It will deceive, steal, cheat, and kill for its thirst is irresistible (Prov. 1:16). It portrays itself to be a friend, a co-worker, a preacher, a counselor; whatever the disguise maybe it depicts a smoothness of malice and hate (Prov. 4:16). It lures you in with its enticements of lust. Before you know, you will have chosen a path of sin that leadeth [continue to lead] into damnation and spiritual apostasy.

Your flesh seeks a love affair, a bond with the world that continually says, "Come, sup with me, come lay with me, come and fornicate with my trappings of enticement" (Prov. 6:18). The flesh cries out daily for sin in as many forms as it comes (Gal. 5:19-21). The flesh seduces as a lady of the evening soliciting money for sexual favors. Not only does the flesh want you to dabble in its lust, but it also wants you to indulge in its forbidden fruits of passion (Rom. 1:27).

Your flesh will tell you that everyone wants to be like you, everyone is doing it, you are number one, you are on top of your game, and every woman and/or man wants to taste your nectar. The imps of darkness whisper to your unnatural desires and tell you to trade your goodness for self-righteousness and conceitedness, your kindness for false niceties, your love for hatred, and your obedience to God for the lust of the flesh (Rom. 1:28-29).

Your desire for your flesh and the world may have caused many to be offended by you. You're despised by your friends and associates, you're hated for your deception and covetousness, and your tact for telling lies is beyond human consumption (Jude 18-21).

How many times have you seen this represented in the building of believers? This beast, this thing, has become the covering of so many professionals in and out of the church. You commune with such people daily, dressed in Armani suits or dripping with expensive jewelry. They enter flaunting the spirit of self-exaltation and perpetuating their personification of who and what they think they are (1 Pet. 2:11-12).

The beast seeks not to hide its agenda, nor will it duck for being exposed for it loves the limelight and being the center of attention. It adores being the first to be recognized and the last to enter a building. It is always looking and lurking for a way to present and showcase the flesh. I am talking about this beast within each of us for if salvation doesn't become a part of our walk then it will continue its terror upon the soul of a man.

Our flesh continues to think of evil deeds to carry out within Christian settings. It disguises itself as a Christian, yet does not hold to any of the principles of Christ; it esteems itself more than it is their brothers and sisters in the Lord. The flesh has and always be about SELF, standing as an enemy to the spirit man which is Christ.

The will of the flesh attempts to buy its way into the trustees' pockets and beds. When this doesn't work, it seeks out those in positions of authority to corrupt. Just as the flesh can insert itself in the body of the church, it can purchase your soul and allegiance (Rom. 3:13-14). It sets up its agenda of "counterfeit Christianity" within the body of believers, using tactics such as confusion, division, jealousy, maliciousness, and seditions. It corrupts the flow of information within the ranks of the believers.

The flesh connives to spread its discourse effectively to foster clicks. When this doesn't work, the flesh seeks those of the same mindset and spread lies, encouraging them to speak of things that are not of edification to set traps with the body of believers (Rom. 3:16-17). Befriending the weaker saints to destroy their joy, hope, and belief in the infallible God, Scripture states it like this: *"For of this sort are they which creep into houses, and lead captive silly women (men) laden with sins, lead away with divers lusts, Ever learning, and never able to come to the knowledge of the truth"* (2 Tim. 3:6-7).

Wearing the costume of Christianity, yet working under an assumed character (hypocrite) as a dedicated worker in the church, it manipulating its mischief and deceit within the various departments as a choreographer sets the ambiance for its dancers. It corrupts church members to vainly profess how spiritually deep they are in the Scriptures and their walk (2 Tim. 3:3-5). The flesh works daily and continues to cloud the minds of the simple with sensuous words. The flesh penetrates every fiber of thought until lust is conceived in an individual's heart and is manifested in his or her behavior.

The scripture states it like this: *"and the sin which doth so easily beset us."* (Heb. 12:1b). Further, it states: *"Ye have not yet resisted unto blood striving against sin"* (Heb. 12:4). In Galatians chapter 5:17 -21, Apostle Paul speaks explicitly: *"For the flesh lusteth* [continues to lust – wanting what is forbidden, what it cannot have, that which is against God] *against the Spirit, and the Spirit against the flesh: and these are contrary the one to the other; so that ye cannot do the things that you would"* (Gal 5:17).

Now in understanding the Word of God we understand that Paul is not writing to the unsaved. He is writing to those who are professing to be a Christian yet still caught up in their carnal flesh. Romans 3:23 says that all have sinned and fallen short of the glory of God, but they are accepted freely by His grace through the redemption of Jesus Christ. Otherwise, the penalty for sin is death (Rom. 6:23). So, even though man sinned, God provided a way to make things right by sending His Son to die and pay the penalty for sin for us.

1. **Pantheism** says there is no guilt because you are a god and just need to recognize it. Through the process of karma and reincarnation, you'll eventually figure it out.

2. **Naturalism** says there is no guilt because you are just responding to external stimuli and your environment made you do it.

Those religions that teach that there is guilt all have an alternate system by which you can earn God's approval. Christianity is unique because it recognizes the guilt and it recognizes we can't do anything about it on our own. Guilt is good because it drives one outside of himself to seek a solution. That solution is Jesus Christ. God has provided a way to take care of our guilt by accepting Christ's payment for this guilt on our behalf.

3. **Universalism**
    I can't help but think that the wide acceptance of universalism is the product of living in a culture where man is not responsible for the crimes he commits.

4. **Pelagianism**
    The founder of Pelagianism, Pelagius. categorically denies the doctrine of original sin, arguing that Adam's sin affected Adam alone and that infants at birth are in the same state as Adam was before the Fall. As such, the belief insists that the constituent nature of humanity is not convertible; it is destructively good.

All his ideas were chiefly rooted in the old, pagan philosophy, especially in the popular system of the Stoics, rather than in Christianity. He regarded the moral strength of man's will when steeled by asceticism as sufficient in itself to attain the loftiest ideal of virtue. The value of Christ's redemption was, in his opinion, limited mainly to instruction and example, which the Savior threw into the balance as a counterweight against Adam's wicked example so that nature retains its ability to conquer sin and gain eternal life even without the aid of God Almighty's grace (Bilson 2020).

How many times have you judged a person on their outward appearance or actions? Do you know that this beast I have explained has presented itself in all of us in our walk as a carnal Christian? The issue is much more problematic than judging based on how much an individual indulges in fleshly sinful acts of pleasure. A person has to recognize that he is a sinner before he sees the need for a Savior. If we are not mindful of our fleshy nature, we will miss heaven and spend eternity in fire and brimstone tormented daily.

Let's stop here once again, for I want to be clear so that none will misconstrue what I am uncovering. The body of a man was created pure and good (Gen .1:31); there was nothing inherently evil or sinful about the man. But according to the Bible, the body is different from the flesh, which in the Scriptures has at least three meanings: the flesh of our physical body (John 6:55); the fallen, corrupted body contaminated by sin (Rom. 7:18); and the fallen man (Rom. 3:20). God did not create fallen flesh; He created a body of flesh, blood, and bones. When man fell, sin, the evil nature of Satan, came into man's body, transmuting it into the flesh. This flesh is called "the flesh of sin" (Rom. 8:3, GK), and the fallen body is called "the body of sin" (Rom. 6:6) and "the body of this death" (Rom. 7:24). Because the God-created body has been corrupted and ruined by sin and transmuted into the flesh, all kinds of lusts are now in the members of our body (Gal. 5:24; Col. 3:5).

Jesus states it like this, *"If any man will come after me, let him deny himself, and take up his cross daily, and follow me. For whosoever will save his life shall lose it: but whosoever will lose his life for my sake, the same shall save it"* (Luke 9:23-24). And, *"therefore if any man be in Christ, he is a new* (regenerate) *creature: old things are passed away' behold* (take note) *(regenerate)"* (2 Cor. 5:17). In another scripture: *"Mortify* (put under subjection, control:) *therefore your members which are upon the earth; fornication, uncleanness, inordinate affection, evil concupiscence, and covetousness, which is idolatry:* (Col. 3:5).

> Without mortifying this beast [the flesh], it will rise up, it will begin to worship itself more and more

(covetousness & idolatry). *"But my people would not hearken to my voice; and Israel would none of me"* (Ps. 18:11).

This beast (the flesh, our nature) will have you doing all kinds of detestable things that separate you from the love of God,. *"So I gave them up unto their own hearts' lust: and they walked in their own counsels"* (Ps. 18:12). Manipulating the Word of God so that you can continue to participate in sinful acts. Studying the Word of God to gainsay not to show yourself approved unto God Almighty. This flesh that works within each of us cannot be tamed by merely saying it with your mouth or even trying to become disciplined in behavior. God is not asking just for your change in behavior (how you do things); but, also your change in nature (heart, which is your attitude). Paul states it this way: *"For which things' sake the wrath of God cometh on the children of disobedience: In the which ye also walked some time, when ye lived in them. But now ye also put off all these; anger, wrath, malice, blasphemy, filthy communication out of your mouth. Lie not one to another, seeing that ye have put off the old man with his deeds; And have put on the new man, which is renewed in knowledge after the image of him that created him"* (Col. 3:6-10).

This beast can only be controlled by the Holy Spirit. Paul stated. *"O wretched man that I am! who shall deliver me from the body of this death?* (Romans 7:24), and he understood that it is through Christ that he saw victory. The nature of flesh only views the things of the world and its master, Satan. *"For all that is in the world, the lust of the flesh, and the lust of the eyes, and the pride of life, is not of the Father, but is of the world"* (1 John 2:16). However, the blood of Jesus Christ, and this alone, saves us and resurrects us from this sinful behavior and the nature of our flesh. *"And the world passeth away, and the lust thereof: but he that doeth the will of God abideth forever"* (1 John 2:17).

The blood of Jesus will rescue, deliver, control, motivate, and move us into a life of victory in and through Him if we just deny or utterly contradict our fleshly nature. Without Christ and denying yourself, you must understand that you are doomed to live the life of destruction of sin and death unto your flesh. Therefore, put off the sin of an evil heart and begin to worship God as He gives you, as written in Ezekiel 36:26, *"A new heart also will I give you, and a new spirit will I put within you: and I will take away the stony heart out of your flesh, and I will give you an heart of flesh."*

The blood of Jesus many speak of is not merely thinking that we receive; it is a reality. It moves the individual into faith, the basis of which is what we believe and all that is in Jesus Christ. Therefore, if we believe that God will give us a new heart and a new spirit, then our behavior and nature will fall in line and be accessible to the move of Christ in our lives. For instance, when you go to the doctor, you are asked to sit down in the waiting room and you don't question whether the chair will hold your weight or not. Romans 12:1 expresses this in detail: *"I beseech you therefore, brethren, by the mercies of God, that ye present your bodies a living sacrifice, holy, acceptable unto God, which is your reasonable service."* It is that simple. Like sitting down in a chair with no thought of whether the chair will break or not, this is what Christ is saying to us as it is the same as giving God yourself as a living sacrifice. Don't think about what you can do, where you can go, what you can watch, what you can eat or drink Just do it and just mortify (cut-off) your deeds of the flesh. Don't rely on how you feel, what you think (don't over analyze), or what it looks like to others. Just deny and mortify this beast.

I want you to understand more than anything the devices of the enemy and his workings in our flesh. We cannot live apart physically from our flesh because this is our make-up, our nature. Nevertheless, we can live apart from the fleshy desires of our flesh and learn to walk in the spirit of God as He shows us how to control and deny this beast.

I remember a time in the ministry when I met a young man who caused me to see this flesh as it is— raw in design. This young man told me he wanted to live for God and he wanted to love God with all of his heart. Then I asked him what was keeping him from loving and living for God? And he stated, "Because, I love the world more!" Those five little words caused me to think harder on the deception of the enemy and his working with our flesh. Some are addicted to the lust of the world like an alcoholic to a bottle of liquor. They are drawn away." *But every man is tempted, when he is drawn away of his own lust, and enticed. Then when lust hath conceived, it bringeth forth sin: and sin, when it is finished, bringeth forth death"* (James 1:14-15). My point is that no matter the addiction—drugs, sex, or seeking attention, etc.— loving the world and all of its deceptions will lead to a life of destruction and one alienated from God the Father. When the flesh is out of control, it is like a nuclear bomb; it does not only engulf and destroy you but everyone around you.

Therefore, the question you truly need to ask is "Is it worth it?" To live a life without Christ as our Saviors is hell by itself for Christ is the One who gives us life and that more abundantly. *"If we confess our sins, he is faithful and just to forgive us our sins, and to cleanse us from all unrighteousness"* (1 John 1:9). We may say we yearn for the emptiness in our heart, mind, and life to be filled, we may even try to live a good life by our behavior for a few weeks or months, but if we do not surrender unto God our sinful nature of thoughts and deeds and mean it from the heart we will continue to go through the motions of trying to control our behavior and never grasp the fulfillment of living for Christ.

"That if thou shalt confess (agree with God) *with thy mouth the Lord Jesus, and shalt believe in thine heart that God hath raised him from the dead, thou shalt be saved"* (Rom. 10:9).

Just going to some meetings, hoping to change your behavior, and standing up saying that I am an alcoholic, drug addict, or a pervert is not enough because these meetings only deal with the flesh of a person. This deception is like saying, "See, I've changed my behavior," yet nature stays the same and that is why the flesh returns to doing those things and ones more damnable things than before. Therefore, it is important that we deal with the natural man and not just his behavior. This is called regeneration or being born again. YOU must be born again! (John 3:3).

The Works of the Flesh

So where do we go from here? Recognizing who and what spirit continues to work in you is the first step. This is not to judge you according to your past sin, but to bring you into an awareness of your flesh and its workings. Satan can only whisper to us the deeds of the flesh, however, when we begin to partake of his words and taste his desires, we sup with him which ultimately will bring forth death. The Bible speaks on this authority that we should yield our members to He we must become a servant too. If we yield our bodies, mind, and soul to the gratification and lust of the flesh, then we are the servant to it.

The Scripture speaks in Matthew 24:6-7 KJV, *"And ye shall hear of wars and rumours of wars: see that ye be not troubled: for all these things must come to pass, but the end is not yet. For nation shall rise against nation, and kingdom against kingdom: and there shall be famines, and pestilences, and earthquakes, in divers places."* Also, in Matthew 10:21 NIV it is written, *"Brother will betray brother to death, and a father his child; children will rebel against their parents and have them put to death."* Luke 12:53 further adds, *"They will be divided, father against son and son against father, mother against daughter and daughter against mother, mother-in-law against daughter-in-law and daughter-in-law against mother-in-law."* This ideology transposes itself into a garment that can easily be worn. It poses as the elite of the elite, the talented of the most talented, the gifted of the most gifted, and so on. It discards those who are loyal and loving and embraces those who despise good and love the flesh. Such belief configures itself like a moonlight sonata on a clear summer night, whispering it in a boisterous tone that you cannot shake. It will not speak of righteous confidence, which is in Christ Jesus your Hope of Glory, but pronounce its stand in colors of deceit as a male peacock uses its beautiful feathers to attract its mate.

Allow me to elaborate. The natural man brings forth the "works of the flesh" (Gal. 5:20-21). These works of the flesh conceal itself in the armor of pride. The works of the flesh manipulate itself for self-importance and it dresses in conceitedness, arrogance, and haughtiness to disguise its maliciousness. Its loins are girted with lies, scheming, and exploitations; its breastplate is layered with hatred and discord; its feet continually run toward fraud and treachery' and its shield is colored with malice and filthiness. Each time this evil soldier moves, it releases a deadly dart that can penetrate the heart of its victim. The Scripture states it like this: *"And the sin which doth so easily beset us"* (Heb.12:1b).

Let's rightly divide the word of God at this point and go to Romans 8:5-8:

> *For they that are after the flesh do mind the things of the flesh; but they that are after the Spirit the things of the Spirit. For to be carnally (of this world) minded is death; but to be spiritually (things of God) minded is*

life and peace. Because the carnal mind is enmity (hostile or hatred – a reason for opposition) against God: for it is not subject to the law (moral) of God, neither indeed can be. So then they that are in the flesh cannot please God."

This flesh moves within the confines of pride in life, confounding souls, taking everyone and their neighbor captive, and striking at inopportune times. It never allows individuals the knowledge of whom and what causes them to drive into the abyss of nothingness. This force grows stronger each day, undermining our every thought and action. This beast that stares at you daily sits among the sinners as well as the saints. He is Pride of Life –. He whispers the selfish desires that do not line up with God's Word and tells you God needs you to be successful and powerful., It labels every destructive desire as the move of God, a new beginning, quoting various scriptures to align its logic of theology. Yet he will never tell you that with Christ you are successful and powerful in Him. You are caught in a vicious cycle of deceit and wanting to be deceived. I call this place "Lodebar" meaning "no pasture" (Biblestudytools.com 2020).

Many have called it other things such as Hell on earth, Wilderness, Nothingness, etc., however, I will express this place as God has explained it to me. It is the place of no WORD, a derogatory name denoting a lack of enlightenment or stupidity. In this place, many men and women find themselves waddling in despair and shame, wanting to be rescued from the humiliation and degradation of the flesh. However, as I embrace the dilemma of this beast that arrays itself in the mirror of life, I know you can escape and be rescued from this place of sin. All that needs be done is embrace the walk of Christ, so vividly expressed in the words of Rev. C. H. Spurgeon *(Dec. 1859): "The more you know of God's attributes, the more you understand of his acts; the more you treasure up of his promises, and the more you fully dive into the depths of his covenant, the more difficult will it become for satan to tempt you to despondency and despair" (Spurgeon 1860, 12).* In short, meditate on His law both day and night. In Psalms1:3 KJV, the Word of God refers to a righteous man like this: *Blessed is the man that walketh not in the counsel of the ungodly, nor standeth in the way of sinners, nor sitteth in the seat of the scornful. But his delight is in the law of the Lord; and in his law doth he meditate day and night. And he shall be like a tree planted by the rivers of water, that bringeth forth his fruit in his season; his leaf also shall not wither; and whatsoever he doeth shall prosper.*

As a person continues to draw closer and see through the eyes of Christ, he will begin to understand Paul as he wrote so eloquently in Hebrews 12:1 KJV: *"Wherefore seeing we also are compassed about with so great a cloud of witnesses, let us lay aside every weight, and the sin which doth so easily beset us, and let us run with patience the race that is set before us."* This beast (sin) that so easily besets is expressed with clarity in Romans 7:15-25 KJV:

> *For that which I do I allow not: for what I would, that do I not; but what I hate, that do I. If then I do that which I would not, I consent unto the law that it is good. Now then it is no more I that do it, but sin that dwelleth in me. For I know that in me (that is, in my flesh), dwelleth no good thing: for to will is present with me; but how to perform that which is good I find not. For the good that I would I do not: but the evil which I would not, that I do. Now if I do that I would not, it is no more I that do it, but sin that dwelleth in me. I find then a law, that, when I would do good, evil*

is present with me. For I delight in the law of God after the inward man: But I see another law in my members, warring against the law of my mind, and bringing me into captivity to the law of sin which is in my members. O wretched man that I am! who shall deliver me from the body of this death? I thank God through Jesus Christ our Lord. So then with the mind I myself serve the law of God, but with the flesh the law of sin."

We can look at the above scriptures as the antidote to addiction to the flesh. Our logical mind would think of addiction as someone who is addicted to a chemical substance or sort; however if we were to analyze –addiction more closely we would find both the physiological and psychological aspects of an addict. The word addict is defined in the Encarta World English Dictionary as: "1) Somebody dependent on the drug – somebody who is physiologically or psychologically dependent on a potentially harmful drug; 2) To devote or give (oneself) habitually or compulsively: she was addicted to soap operas; 3) A devoted believer or follower: we are all addicts of change" (Encarta World English Dictionary 2000).

By no means do I ascribe to the clinical state of theoretical psychology, however, we know an addict who is chemically dependent upon the drug does not have full control of him or herself. The substance has control of their thoughts and actions. The addict cannot resist the taste, smell, and sight of their drug of choice because the dependence and cravings are so strong that they overpower any logical thinking. The obsession is so psychologically embedded into the psychic that the desire and lust become one with the individual so that nothing else matters.

Following the second and third definitions above, anything that has control over you that you have no control over becomes the overpowering force in your life. More so than the first definition, they refer to something you habitually give yourself too. This is the besetting of which Hebrews 12:1 speaks. Beset means 1) to attack from all sides; 2) to trouble persistently, harass; or 3) to hem in, surround (The Free Dictionary 2020). The word besetting sin means a continual troubling or vexing (Merriam-Webster Dictionary 2020). Whatsoever thing that is controlling you and has the best of you is the sin (*Wherefore seeing we also are compassed about with so great a cloud of witnesses, let us lay aside every weight, and the sin which doth so easily beset us, and let us run with patience the race that is set before us,* (Hebrew 12:1). To make it plain, the sin you keep falling into, the lifestyle, and the habitual hauntings you try to stop through starvation tactics, Paul brings to light in Romans chapter 7. He presents a picture of a sin that keeps tormenting and causing one to do what they do not want to do. This conceptual evidence is why so many altars, are full with many struggling to rid themselves of things that have control over them. Paul struggled to free himself of something that had control over him, and addiction, that he could not free himself from. He identified the problem, short and simple, as "sin" that was dwelling within him (Romans 7:20, 23). Truthfully, all addiction is sin.

The Greek word that refers to sin is translated in John 8:11 as "to miss the mark (as to not share in the prize). Philippians 3:14 KJV states what your action should be instead: "*I press toward the mark for the prize of the high calling of God in Christ Jesus*". The reality is that when you are addicted to something, it will cause you to miss the mark God has set for you. The addiction causes you to turn your attention from where the Lord wants you to be; you know, as in taking your eyes off of the prize (Jesus Christ).

Most addictions are born out of a sense of desperation, whether one possesses low self-esteem or high self-esteem. When believers realize they have a problem with a besetting sin (troubling, persistent sin) that is overpowering them, they normally seek out avenues to help them cope, such as reading books, listening to recordings, seeking counseling, and engaging themselves in spiritual activities to find freedom and peace. But, despite these efforts, most wind up still addicted, time after time running to the altar requesting prayer, going through this ritual and that to no avail, even convincing themselves that God is not real Finally after all realization has seeped from their conscience, they find themselves no better off than before. They may overcome addiction in one area of their lives, but overall, they find themselves still trapped in a new area. Hopeless though they have strived and labored, they come to the place Paul describes so articulately in the passage of Romans 7 I shared above.

As followers of Christ the Savior, we must realize the sin of self, stating, 'I can't defeat this thing. It's bigger than I am, I give up, and I am hopelessly addicted and enslaved to it." This place of self-loathing is just where one needs to be, the very place that the Lord wants you to come too—the end of yourself, the place where you abhor everything that you have become and done. If you never come to this place, you will never be set free from your addiction, your bondage of sin.

Paul comes finally to the conclusion that the answer which seems so far away is just at reach. *"Oh wretched* (inferior, despicable, worthless, shameful, inadequate) *man that I am* (what dilemma, quandary, difficulty, a mess I am in), *who will set me free from* (my slavery to) *sin* – (habits, from the desires of my fleshly self-life) – who can…who can deliver me from this body of death? There is only One who can. However, until you come to the absolute end of self and the end of your, you will never find freedom from your addictions.

Endless Thoughts of Time

And take heed to yourselves, lest at any time your hearts be overcharged with surfeiting, and drunkenness, and cares of this life, and so that day come upon you unawares. For as a snare shall it come on all them that dwell on the face of the whole earth. Luke 21:34-35 KJV.

We live in a time when men run to and from. Knowledge is increased, yet it is seemingly harder and harder to find the knowledge of God. The Scriptures tell us not to get caught up in the cares of life for, if we are obedient to God, He will take care of all of our needs. Yet, we tell ourselves it is hard to live for God when we have so much going on. In other words, it is hard to live for God when you are living for yourself. Scripture state: *"And take heed to yourselves, lest at any time your hearts be overcharged"* (Luke 21:34 KJV).

So why do we become overwhelmed by our struggles in life? *And take heed to yourselves, lest at any time your hearts be overcharged with surfeiting, and drunkenness, and cares of this life, and so that day come upon you unawares* (Luke 21:34 KJV). I have found that when we allow our care for the things of this world to become our forethought, we become stressed out and ineffective for God. And this is when our soul becomes in danger. In God's Word, He states *"No man can serve two masters: for either he will hate the one and love the other; or else he will hold to the one, and despise the other. Ye cannot serve God and mammon"* (Matt. 6:24 KJV). So, in theory, you will love either God or the world, but you cannot love both. To say one believes and does the opposite. it would be safe to say they do not believe. However, God has a way of bringing you back to yourself. When you reach the fork in the road of your mind, God has a way of putting you back on the straight and narrow road and not the path that leads to destruction. I understand it may take someone day or other twenty years to learn to completely trust the all Wise and Living God without any doubts that He truly cares for us. In those seven years of famine and drought, God was still prevalent. He is moving in our lives as He did then, causing His complete will to be done as passersby look upon our flesh as broken and torn.

I am not here to glorify sin nor the devices the enemy uses to achieve the ultimate satisfaction of destroying the very temple of God with the lust of the flesh and the pride of life. But, we need to understand the lust of the flesh for we deal with it daily.

Below is a picture from Charles's Larkin (1921) that accurately describes the workings of the flesh.

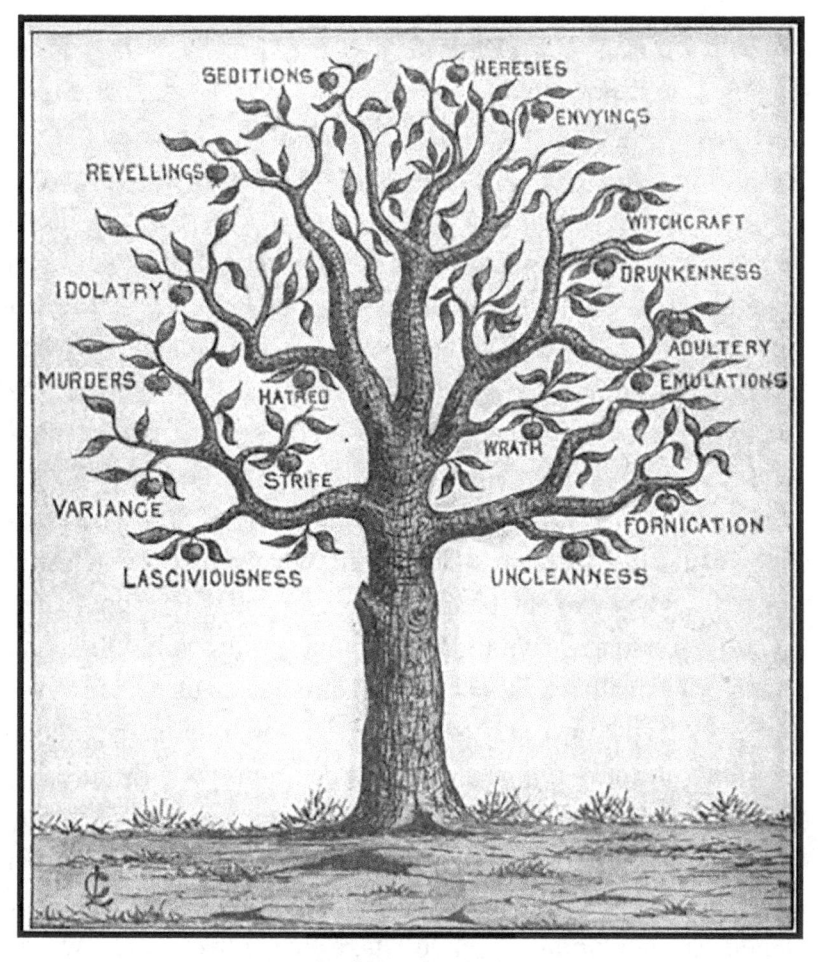

(Larkin 1921, 212).

Living the Christian life means deliverance from trouble, hardship, pain, and disappointments. It is deliverance in difficult times, which brings us to the reality of knowing who God is in our life. *"He that dwelleth in the secret place of the Most High...there shall no evil befall thee"* (Ps. 91). No problem, no situation, no circumstance can come to nigh the place where you are at one with God. If you are a child of God, there certainly will be troubles to meet you, but Jesus says do not be surprised when they come. *Beloved, think it not strange concerning the fiery trial which is to try you, as though some strange thing happened unto you:* (1 Peter 4:12) God does not give us overcoming life; He gives us life as we overcome. *And they overcame him by the blood of the Lamb, and by the word of their testimony; and they loved not their lives unto the death* (Rev. 12:11). The strain is strength. If there is no strain, there is no strength. Think about it. Are you asking God to give you, life, liberty, and joy? If so, we must accept the strain. Immediately when you face the strain, you will get the strength. *"For the joy of the Lord is our strength"* (Neh. 8:10c). Overcome your circumstances, pains, and confusion by taking the first step to the Lord. *"Come unto me, all ye that labour and are heavy laden, and I will give you rest"* (Matt 11:28). Overcome your timidity and take the step, and God will give you to eat the tree of life and you will be nourished. If you continue to strive to do it in your ability, you will spend yourself physically out of control, becoming exhausted. However, if you *"But seek ye first the kingdom of God, and his righteousness; and all these things shall be added unto you"* (Matt 6:33) spiritually you will gain more strength. Do you know God not only gives you strength for tomorrow, or the next hours, or for the strain of the moment? The temptation is to face difficulties from a common-sense standpoint. We should take solace from God's words, *"I can do all things through Christ which strengthens me"* (Phil. 4:13). Only then will we realize the importance of going through difficulties when we see God as the "Problem Solver."

Peter–The Example

I'm reminded of Peter in the Word of God.

> *"And the Lord turned, and looked upon Peter...and Peter went out, and wept bitterly"* (Luke 22:61-62).

Every man at some time has fallen in his life, and usually more than once. We have all thought how could Peter deny Christ, but let's closer Peter's actions. Many make excuses for their lack of faith and disbelief for they know it was so with Peter. They follow the same dreary stage in life, missing every opportunity to recommit, resubmit, and repent to the hand of God. Was it faithlessness that made him follow Christ afar off, instead of keeping at his Master's side. Or maybe if Peter would have watched and prayed and not sleep while in the garden, things would have been different. But no, this was Peter's destiny, to know that the heart is deceitful above all things. To live so long in the inner circle of fellowship with Christ, as one of that most select audience who witnessed the glory of the transfiguration who had witnessed the most solemn words the world had ever heard, how could he have turned his back upon his Lord? The question must have crossed Peter's mind; "What have I done?"

But there is a greater fact in Peter's life. He repented. All the world is at one with Peter in his sin, but not all the world is with him in his repentance. Just at for you, sin loves company but *"Righteousness exalteth a nation: but sin is a reproach to any people"* (Prov. 14:34 KJV). The real lesson of Peter's life is the lesson in repentance. His fall is a lesson in sin, which requires no teacher, but his repentance is a great lesson in salvation. And Peter's repentance (penitence) is a great lesson in salvation.

The life true story of Peter's sin may be defined as the ideal progress of Christian repentance. We find here four outstanding characteristics of the state of penitence:

1) Divine: It began with God. Peter did not turn. But *"the Lord turned and looked upon Peter."* (Luke 22:61).

2) Sensitive: *"The Lord looked upon Peter."*

3) Intense: *"Peter went out and wept bitterly."*

4) Lonely: *"Peter went out"* out into the quiet night to be alone with his sin and God.

These are characteristic not only of the penitential state but of all God's operations on the soul.

To take the first of these, we find that at the beginning of this strange experience came from God. It was not Peter who turned. The Lord turned and looked upon Peter. When the cock crowed, it was a signal that Peter might have recalled him to himself. But he was just in the very act of sin. And when a man is in the thick of his sin, his last thought is to throw down his arms and repent. So, Peter never thought of turning, but the Lord turned; and when Peter would rather have looked anywhere else than at the Lord, the Lord looked at Peter.

Now the result of this distinction is this: the revelation that there are two kinds of sorrow for sin and these are different in their origin, religious value, and influence on our life. The lighter kind is when a man does wrong, and, in the ordinary sense of the word, is sorry that he has done it. We count this feeling of reproach which treads so closely on the act of compensation or atonement for the wrong. This is a kind of sorrow that is well known to all who examine themselves and in any way struggle with sin. It is a kind of sorrow that gives relief to what is called a penitential heart. But it is a startling truth that there is no real penitence there, no true sorrow for sin. All that is revealed is wounded self-love. This wounded self-love merely reflects the pride in the individual—that he did not do better, that he was not as good as he deceived himself or his neighbor. In reality, it is as if Peter turned and looked at himself in the mirror to see the beast that he truly was. For when Peter turned and looked upon himself, he saw the poor, weak, spineless creature that he was. Have you ever wondered what would have happened if God had not looked upon Peter? He might have wept more bitterly, not because he had sinned against his God, but because he, the great disciple, had done a weak thing—that he was weak as other men.

The disgrace or low in the spirit that comes to us when we find ourselves overtaken in a fault is often nothing more than a vexation and an annoyance with ourselves, that after all our good resolutions and attempts at reformation, we have broken down again.

Let's look at another case that contrasts the publican's prayer of penitence in the temple who did not have wounded pride, when he cried out to the Lord, *"God be merciful to me, a sinner!"* (Luke 18:13c). Stricken before his God, this publican had little thought of the self-respect he had lost and felt it no indignity in taking the culprit's place and being taught the true divinity of a culprit's penitence.

Can you not see the difference between the publican's penitence and Peter's penitence? this is the difference between the divine and the human. The one is God turning and looking upon man, the other is man turning and looking upon himself. There is no wrong in a man turning and looking upon himself; only there is danger. There is the danger of misinterpreting what he sees and feels. What he feels is the mortification, the self-reproach of a sculptor who has made an unlucky stroke of the chisel; the changing of the artist who has spoiled the work of weeks by a clumsy touch.

The true aspect of having a form of religion is that we must feel mortified when we do wrong, expressing godly sorrow. Without true penitence, the effect is that self gets into what ought to be the most genuine experience of life and makes an imitation of it, transforming the greatest opportunities for recovery into the basest ministry to pride. The true experience, on the other hand, is a touching lesson in human helplessness, teaching that shows that God has to come to man's relief at every turn of his life, and how the same Hand which provides His pardon has actually to draw him to the place of repentance.

It is only God who looks into the heart of a sinner who shows forth the sacrifice of a broken and contrite heart. As we look like Luke's account of the prodigal son's life, *"He came to himself,"* and then *"he came to his father."* (Luke 15:17). This expresses the process of how we come to ourselves. We as God's children are always finding out, like the prodigal, the miserable covenants/deals we have made. But it is only when we come to our Father that we can get them undone and the real debt discharged.

Let's complete the thought of how the Lord turned and looked upon Peter. As I ponder on this, I only can think of the sensitivity that Christ had upon Peter. Peter was perhaps the most assertive of all the disciples. He was a man that may have been strong-built, robust, fearless in disposition tough quick-tempered, and rash, and a man who would rant and swear. However, as Peter swears with his lips, I'm sure there was dead silence in his soul. An emptiness, a void—the remembrance of the words of Christ—permeated into the thoughts of sorrow and pain. Then the Lord turned and looked. A look and that was all. The sincere, piercing look from Jesus rent through his heart as lightning strikes a tree leaving its impression upon the heart of his very soul. A man that was shaped in intolerance, bigotry and prejudiced was made into a man of righteousness and a conduit of Christ, the Hope, and Restoration.

Chapter 14

THE STATE OF MAN

The normal state of man is written in Psalm 14:2-3 KJV): *"The Lord looked down from heaven upon the children of men, to see if there were any that did understand, and seek God. They are all gone aside, they are all together become filthy: there is none that doeth good, no, not one."* Isaiah 64:6 KJV offers more: *"But we are all as an unclean thing, and all our righteousness are as filthy rags; and we all do fade as a leaf; and our iniquities, like the wind, have taken us away.* These words of life can only be applied when one believes that in Christ there is hope. However, they can be hard to grasp, especially if you think you can help yourself or have so much confidence in your ability, strength, and resources, and education.

When you come to the end of self, these verses take on life and that more abundantly. Many people quote these verses and refer them, but others never take into account their application to themselves due to their pride and ego. But if you are to be delivered, this antidote must be indigested daily if you will be freed from the addictive penchants in your life.

Seriously, nothing you can do or say can buy the love of God into your life, for it is because He first proved and established His love to and for you. *"The Lord hath appeared of old unto me, saying, Yea, I have loved thee with an everlasting love: therefore with loving kindness have I drawn thee"* (Jer. 31:3 KJV). *"I led them with cords of human kindness, with ties of love; I lifted the yoke from their neck and bent down to feed them"* (Hosea 11:4 KJV). Jesus came to you and rescued you while you were running the other way, not to Him, but from Him. He courted you by His Spirit when you were a sinner and drew you closer and closer to Himself. He saved you, and now He continues to pursue you with His loving kindness though you continue to fight and kick. Yet the scriptures cry out in a perpetual calling: *"There is none that understandeth, there is none that seeketh after God"* (Rom. 3:11 KJV); *"For the people turneth not unto him that smiteth them, neither do they seek the Lord of hosts (Isa. 9:13); and "For the Son of man is come to seek and to save that which was lost"* (Luke 19:10 KJV). We are like sheep; *"All we like sheep have gone astray; we have turned everyone to his own way; and the Lord hat laid on him the iniquity of us all"* (Isa. 53:6 KJV).

Can you see how our looking God in the face daily, receiving His blessings, love, grace, and mercy, but saying with our actions "whatever" or "so what," is just as the story of Esau and Jacob? The bargain made between Jacob and Esau about the "rite," it was Esau's by birth, but Jacob's by promise; it was a spiritual privilege. But Jacob sought to obtain the birthright by crooked courses flamed by selfish desire. He coveted earnestly the best gifts; he was wrong in taking advantage of his brother's need. Jacob's pottage pleased Esau's eye. Esau was gratifying the sensual appetite of his palate, yet this same sensual appetite continues to ruin thousands of precious souls through its addictions. Romans 16:18 KJV says, *"For they that are such serve not our Lord Jesus Christ, but their own belly; and by good words and fair speeches deceive the hearts of the simple."* – Men's hearts are walking after their own lust of eyes according to Job 31:7 KJV: *"If my step hath turned out of the way, and mine heart walked after mine eyes, and if any blot hath cleaved to mine hands."* When men serve their own bellies, they are sure to be punished.

This etymology of profaneness, with which Paul patented Esau in Hebrews 12:16 KJV —*"Lest there [be] any fornicator, or profane person, as Esau, who for one morsel of meat sold his birthright"*—is the greatest folly. It is a travesty to part with our blessings and inheritance in God the Father and Jesus the Son of God, our Redeemer, and in heaven for the riches, honors, and pleasures of this world as though it was a morsel of sell. Esau ate and drank, satisfied his appetite, and then carelessly rose and went his way without any serious thought about what he had done nor with regret over the bargain he had made for his flesh.

Thus, Esau despised his birthright. By his neglect and contempt afterward, and by justifying himself in what he had done, he put the bargain past recall. People are ruined, not so much by doing what is inappropriate or wrong but by doing it and not repenting of it. Where do you fall? Are you riding high with no thoughts of what today will bring?

When confronted by Jacob's porridge soup, Esau said, I'll sell my inheritance forever, for a little monetary porridge (Gen 25:30-33). Just as probably you have thought, he must have been crazy to give up his inheritance for a little meat. But have you considered how easily you can sell your birthright, your God-given inheritance, for something as temporal and worthless as a piece of meat?

This problem of our human nature was described in Jeremiah 17:5-6 KJV: *"Thus saith the LORD; Cursed be the man that trusteth in man, and maketh flesh his arm, and whose heart departeth from the LORD. For he shall be like the heath in the desert and shall not see when good cometh; but shall inhabit the parched places in the wilderness, in a salt land and not inhabited."* In verses 7-8, Jeremiah paints a portrait of sovereignty, peace, and prosperity—a landscape where the tree is planted by the waters and nothing can befall its placement there; *"Blessed is the man that trusteth in the LORD, and whose hope the LORD is. For he shall be as a tree planted by the waters, and that spreadeth out her roots by the river, and shall not see when heat cometh, but her leaf shall be green; and shall not be careful in the year of drought, neither shall cease from yielding fruit.".* By the time we get to verse 9, he reiterates human nature once again: *"The heart is deceitful above all things, and desperately wicked: who can know it?"* This cry once again resurfaces in Paul's account in Roman 7:24, and I repeat, *"O wretched man that I am? Who shall deliver me from the body of this death."*

One of the keys to freedom from bondage is within the revelation of death to self (to deny oneself – see Chapter 4). There is no other way to escape damnation but through Jesus Christ. You must come to the end of yourself and cry out to God. You must know and fully believe nothing else and no one else can ever extricate you from your bondage. Not shaking of the pastor's hand, not working diligently in the ministry, not going to confessions. It is only after you truly acknowledge your hopeless fleshly addiction and genuinely turn to the Lord for deliverance that will you find it.

Let me share what Jeremiah tells of as God spoke clearly to him: *"I the LORD search the heart, I try the reins, even to give every man according to his ways, and according to the fruit of his doings"* (Jer. 17:10). *"I try the reins"* means the mind or inner self. Further down in verse 14, Jeremiah understood his inadequacy and then cried out from the depths of his heart as only one in bondage desiring deliverance can do: *"Heal me, O LORD, and I shall be healed; save me, and I shall be saved: for thou art my praise."*

The Shadow of Hell

Hell is just a mere reflection of one's existence. It shapes itself into an ideal of symbols, signs, allegories, moments, and facets of reality. It has no exact season or exactness of time. Yet in its wings of depression, it stalks its prey like a tiger stalking a prey; when it hits, it leaves you weak and vulnerable to its devices of the flesh. Its tentacles of mind control preach failure, defeat, and destruction. Its melodies of romantic seductions rustle softly bringing hate, malice, and deceit to your very being.

Hell is not a welcome friend. You cannot hide nor can run when the shadows of hell come within your being. From every corner, it preaches from the pulpit of lies and deceit. This shadow of hell doesn't cry out to you, but it wakes you in the middle of the night with its ominous gloom clouds of doubts and confusion. It lurks within the partitions of one's heart to devour and destroy at any given moment. In a twinkling of time, it pounces proudly, placing its disbelief on every circumstance, situation, and problem. Hell supersedes the forefront of thoughts, ideas, and conclusions so that logic no longer makes itself known as wisdom and consciousness becomes void of understanding. None are safe from falling into its grip.

This shadow of hell continues to beat upon your existence until you surrender to its will. It pressures one to its knees like an armed robber slowly yet surely points his gun at the innocent head of a child. As you stare into the mouth of the void, grasping for a breath of hope, you can only cry out once again, "Lord save me."

As these shadows of hell continue to press upon your heart, a haunting feeling of panic overcomes you and at that moment you'll see that you have fallen into the abyss of self-depravity and self-loathing. The shadow has brought a shame of despair with its long tentacles embracing you like a long, lost love embracing moments of passion.

Oh, how sweet the sound of deliverance as it knocks at the door of your heart. Yet you find yourself not able to obtain nor even understand this darkness that continues to follow you, plaguing your thoughts, destroying your deeds, and perpetrating your walk. You strive to be ever learning, but you are not able to grasp a hold on reality. All around you, darkness continues to shadow your mind with thoughts of suicide.

The shadows of death and hell strive to sup with your being—though you refuse so readily, though you protest so vehemently—until you find yourself sitting and tasting its bitter nectar of familiarity. You are left asking yourself why has God forsaken you and knowing that the shadows have besieged you with hopelessness. Feelings of doubts force its question of faith, for the resentment of self-hate and the torment of loneliness has overshadowed you and left you for naught.

Sisters and brothers, I can truly say that I have experienced this shadow of hell. As I write now, I remember speaking of the memories of the love and joy that once brewed from my lips and soul, but looking upon my flesh that had become dejected and dry of life. I thought of how blessings had once spawned from it. A well that had flown with the promises of the Savior had now become dry bones. The fountain that spewed the words of life had become unproductive and no longer gave substance. I thought, "Oh bitter pill from the bowels of hell, cease your torment so that my palate once again can taste honey and bring forth the praise that lays in the hollows of my soul." I began to pray consistently and constantly, asking God once again to allow me to eat of His law. "Allow me to foretell Your wonders so that I may digest Your hope and faith. For you are, oh Lord, the flower of all life and that more abundantly. For you are my Lord, the substance that sustains all life and who I shall partake of forevermore. AMEN."

Chapter 15

SPIRITUAL DISCIPLINE VS. ADDICTIONS

How can one leave a life of fullness, victory, and complete deliverance? Is it an onetime discipline? Can one truly escape their addictions or do we just pick up little "pet sins" to replace the life of self-destruction? This section is to all of you who feel that they are trapped and cannot escape their addictions, whether it is self-afflicted or not, that there is an escape.

However, to rescue you from your wild ways of destruction, you must give your life over to Christ who is the Lord and Master of your life so He can control, direct and teach you how to walk uprightly before Him. Without a consistent, disciplined lifestyle, you will never really be free from your addictive tendencies. Many have stated they do not desire any type of entity controlling them, but I beg the differ. If it is not yourself and your destructive tendencies, it is something else. No matter that you don't want to be controlled, you will either be drawn away by your lust or be nurtured and strengthened by the mighty hand of God through an ordered lifestyle of self-denial and a strong endearing relationship with Jesus the Savior of your soul. The fact is that you must come under the authority of God and be accountable for your thoughts and actions. Do you know that compulsive activity comes when we allow our guards to become so relaxed that we compromise the very thought of who and what God is in our life?

Those compromises are the traps in our lives that come to destroy our God-centeredness. Discipline is the answer in keeping one's mind and heart focused upon the will and way of God. Don't let you are doing so be out of desperation of hope, but a wiliness of mind to follow Christ. Don't let freedom be another ideology of thought bound to the sinful habits that snuff out all basis of reality within you. Freedom is just a call away, and you can have this life full of love, temperance, hope, and faith in the body of Christ even while going through the pressures of life and its hard tribulations.

I must say that deliverance is not a quick fix that immediately frees you from the bondage of life-time abuse and addiction, though I have known many who were delivered instantly from a fraction of their addiction. It is based upon your dedication to your deliverance. It is based on your faith and your action to move forward daily to stay clean from that addictive sin. That means when it seems at times you cannot escape the horrors of the nightmarish flashbacks, you still must face the demons and realize they have no control over your flesh, your mind, or your soul.

Picking up pet sins to replace the demons that torment you, I must remind you that the short term pleasure they provide is a strong residual effect that will cost you to be hell-bound. You have to ask yourself if it is worth throwing away a lifetime of victory in Christ Jesus. This is not to condemn you of what destruction you have chosen to afflict yourself with; sin is sin. It doesn't matter whether it is gluttony, alcoholism, sex, drugs, lying, or stealing, the addiction you want to hold on to will lead you back into a roller-coaster life of unforgiveness that will block your honest repentance. Those small foxes, those small vines, those pet sins, no matter how many, that take the place of faith in your life. Do be like those people who seem to receive their deliverance and picks up other sins that separate them from the love of God. The scripture puts it this way about their hearts being swept clean:

> *When the unclean spirit is gone out of a man, he walketh through dry places, seeking rest, and findeth none. Then he saith, I will return into my house from whence I came out; and when he comes, he findeth it empty, swept, and garnished. Then goeth he, and taketh with himself seven other spirits more wicked than himself, and they enter in and dwell there: and the last state of that man is worse than the first. Even so, shall it be also unto this wicked generation. Matthew 12:43-45 KJV*

Getting saved is not a quick drive-thru deliverance. Many ministries operate this way. They have a "touch and go" approach to salvation; If I've shaken your hand and accepted you as a member, quoted scripture over you, then– you are saved. This is not deliverance nor is it salvation. The key is to stray off unto some itching and follow some doctrine that has no substance or life. Water down an exhibition of deliverance will leave you still struggling with insecurities, despondency, and despair, still looking for answers and searching for a way to escape. Reaming exposed to the hurts and wounds leaves you vulnerable to a Band-Aid effect of a hypocritical attitude.

Do not deceive yourself and allow others to manipulate you into the "I am alright" syndrome. Many people today are dealing with suicidal tendencies that mire them in self-hate. Such an individual needs to be cleaned from within and without; behaviors need to be dealt with as well as an attitude. The whole individual must join with and only Christ. Only Jesus Christ can free one from such a horrific thought. This person needs to undergo a soul surgery, allowing our Lord to break up the fallow ground and give a heart of flesh. This is why spiritual discipline is so important when receiving any type of deliverance.

Functioning in the spiritual discipline must be maintained daily after being received. One must develop a daily walk of consistent prayer (talking and listening to God), a devotional time before the Lord (meditating, studying, and applying the Word), and speaking praise to God throughout the day. This is crucial to maintaining a walk in the Spirit as well as repenting for things that we do, both those that we know not and those things that we do know. For example, David, a man after God's own heart, overcame his addictive tendencies by doing what it says in Psalms 119: 9-16:

> *Wherewithal shall a young man cleanse his way? by taking heed thereto according to thy word. With my whole heart have I sought thee: O let me not wander from thy commandments. Thy word have I hid in mine heart, that I might not sin against thee. Blessed art thou, O LORD: teach me thy statutes. With my lips have I declared all the judgments of thy mouth. I have rejoiced in the way of thy testimonies, as much as in all riches. I will meditate in thy precepts and have respect unto thy ways. I will delight myself in thy statutes: I will not forget thy word.*

Hiding God's word in your heart so you won't sin against Him goes back to Matthew 11:28-30. it is important to keep learning of God. The word "learn," in the Greek "manthano," means "to learn, be apprised: to increase one's knowledge, to be increased in knowledge; to hear, be informed; to learn by use and practice: to be in the habit of, accustomed to" (Thayer 2017, 3129). In short, it means to understand, retain, and master.

In learning of Him and being a disciple of Christ, you must understand His true character is not as the dictatorial tyrant that must be served in the fleshly state. He is a God who is truly concerned about you as His child. God is not like us who can be bought and sold nor does His character rest in pride. Frankly, *"God resists the proud and gives grace to the humble"* (1 Peter 5:5). Therefore, this beast that so easily beset us is the one that we must mortify of its prideful and self-sufficient ways it so readily aligns itself with.

Psychologists typically say pride is an outward manifestation of inward rebellion, resentment, and bitterness. So many people become involved in sinful practices because of pride and the void in their souls due to resisting what makes them miserable within, causing them to fall back to their sinful ways. These addictions cover-up the pain, frustrations, and discontent of They hide behind a costume of unrest, hoping somehow to fill the emptiness with things of this world that do not matter.

Many have been taught that God is only loving and God will never destroy. He is both a God of love and a God of wrath, but it is not God who destroys us; it is ourselves due to this beast of pride wrapped in our flesh. Many of us, when we come to Christ, have never been told or taught that there has to be a life of spiritual discipline and self-denial. Not knowing this, they soon become disillusioned and lose their footing in God. Instead of the rivers of living water flowing through them, they suffer a life of thorns, hardship, pain. Frustrated with a false Christian experience, they turn to their fleshy desires.

Again, I bring to you a way out—JESUS. When you get sick and tired of being sick and tired, or when you simply decide to take God at His Word and move in faith, then will you find yourself coming to Him in humility, repentance, and adoration. Only then will you say, "YES." Reaching the bottom of the pit has a way of opening your heart to the realization of the liberty and power that comes from walking in the Spirit with discipline.

This is where you find the rest that was spoken of before. Rest, my brothers and sisters. In the verse above, the Greek translation contains the word, "anapausis." which means intermission (Mickelson Strong's Concordance 2015, 372). The equivalent in English is the word "respite",' which means a respite or a reprieve (Your Vocabulary Building & Communication Training Center 2007) With this wisdom, we are to believe that this promise of coming to Jesus, picking up your cross daily (spiritual discipline), and understanding His character, will give you from Him a reprieve from the demons of your compulsions as well as complete and total rest from them. That's deliverance; being rescue from oneself. Jesus promised that He will give you rest This rest begets brings hope just as the Scripture states in Romans 6:14: *"For sin shall not have dominion over you: for ye are not under the law but under grace."*

Consider the enigma of this. You must understand in your heart that you have no strength within yourself to break free from your addictions; simply you must come to the end of yourself. Then, at that point, the promise that of the scripture, which declares you have the victory and the power to overcome, begins to have meaning in your experience. Philippians 4:13 confers to us, *"I can do all things through Christ which strengtheneth me"* while Romans 8:38 shares, *"For I am persuaded, that neither death, nor life, nor angels, nor principalities, nor powers, nor things present, nor things to come,* and 1 John 4:4 boast, *"Ye are of God, little children, and have overcome them: because greater is he that is in you, than he that is in the world."*

Chapter 16

FREEDOM FROM BONDAGE

The testimony comes when you stand boldly, confessing who Christ and who He is in your life. Then, God begins giving you a revelation of who He is (His meek and lowly character) and who you are in Him because of Calvary (*"There is therefore now no condemnation to them which are in Christ Jesus, who walk not after the flesh, but after the Spirit"* Rom. 8:1). Oh, what power of this revelation to find the strength in your spirit to stand up and fight against your sin and overcome them all. Yes, my brothers and sisters, it's just that easy; what makes it seem hard is the enemy who is an accuser of the brethren (– *"And I heard a loud voice saying in heaven, Now is come salvation, and strength, and the kingdom of our God, and the power of his Christ: for the accuser of our brethren is cast down, which accused them before our God day and night"* Rev. 12:10). Those enslaving habits and drives are gone, just as Proverbs 13:15 says, *"Good understanding giveth favour: but the way of transgressor is hard."*

The enemy of your soul (your flesh) that wants to keep you bound to your old nature of self-want and self-hate. Even as excuses permeate your soul — "It's too hard," It's too complicated", " He won't forgive me", "I'll never get free"—stop and say right now, "The devil is a liar and the father of all lies; he is a thief and a robber; get thee hence from me." Stop listening to his deception. God told us in Ephesians 4:27 to *"Neither give place to the devil."* James 4:7 encourages us to, *"Submit yourselves therefore to God. Resist the devil, and he will flee from you"*. 1 Peter 5:6-9 directs:

> *Humble yourselves, therefore, under God's mighty hand, that he may lift you up in due time. Cast all your anxiety on him because he cares for you. Be self-controlled and alert. Your enemy the devil prowls around like a roaring lion looking for someone to devour. Resist him, standing firm in the faith, because you know that your brothers throughout the world are undergoing the same kind of sufferings."*

If you listen to Satan, like he deceived Eve, he will continue to deceive you and talk you out of your deliverance. It's your choice. Choose today to be delivered to be free. Deny!

To understand this concept of freedom, you must realize who you war with daily with before you attempt to change it. What will it take for you to see it is not within your power or your authority? –It is God who is telling you that through Him only can you receive this help, this rescue, this deliverance. With this acknowledgment, Jeremiah could then cry for the Lord to heal and save him. Even as I think now, there are so many scriptures celebrating life racing through my heart:

> *"The righteous cry, and the LORD heareth, and delivereth them out of all their troubles"* (Ps. 34:17 KJV).

> *"I sought the LORD, and he answered me; he delivered me from all my fears"* (Ps. 34:6 NIV)

David's life shows you can call unto the Lord and He will hear you; He will save you out of all your troubles. Scripture states that when you cry out, and it comes from deep within, God will hear you. – It is not that the real meaning of the verse *"Whosoever calls upon the name of the Lord shall be saved"* (Rom.10:13)? It must be your cry from the depths of your heart—not others crying out for you—it is– "Lord, help me, save me, deliver me." It is only after repentance has rooted in your heart and mind that your godly sorrow will penetrate the ears of God Almighty to bring for His rescue of you, His child. Can't you see it? Just as your parents responded to your calls of help, so God, in all His loving kindness, reaches down to pull you out of your darkened pit.

In the perception of loving-kindness Jesus gives, He ordained a remedy from our sinful, addictive habits. *"Come unto me, all ye that labour and are heavy laden, and I will give you rest"* (Matt. 11:28 KJV). The word "labor" in the Greek "kopiao", kop-ee-ah'-o" means "fatigued, worn out, or beating your chest in grief." (Blue Letter Bible 2020). The Greek word for "rest" means "to take ease or refresh, a refreshing release" (StudyLight.org 2020). Many of us spend so much time beating ourselves down for those addictive things that are compulsive and habitual. This blocks us from letting God bring us into His fold. God loves us so much that He will not allow you to find hope and lasting liberty without Him for He is a jealous God and will not share His glory with anything else.

Deuteronomy 5: 8-9 states, *"Thou shalt not make thee any graven image, or any likeness of anything that is in heave above, or that is in the earth beneath, or that is in the waters beneath the earth: Thou shalt not bow down thyself unto them, nor serve them: for I the Lord thy God am a jealous God, visiting the iniquity of the fathers upon the children unto the third and fourth generation of them that hate me."*

How would you feel if your loved one gave honor, respect, and adoration to someone else who has done nothing for them while you were there in their back-breaking, tearful, and financially bankrupt circumstances? Though you cannot deliver those in your life, just as they cannot deliver you, is a person, a friend, a lover, a God that surpasses all gods. Jesus is the answer, the way, and the door; He is your Deliverer, your King of King and Lord of Lords.

However, just as Deuteronomy expresses the true divineness of God, Isaiah 42:8 echoes the same thought: *"I am the Lord: that is my name: and my glory will I not give to another, neither my praise to graven images."* With God, all things are possible; He is the only one that can, will, and surely deliver you out of every evil characteristic that dwells within your mortal being. This thought we must ponder and come to grips that it is He (Christ) to whom we must give obedience, allegiance, and reverence *"For God so loved the world* (Greek: kosmos-orderly arrangement Strongs's #2889: kosmos–Greek/Hebrew Definitions–Bible Tools 2020) *that He gave His only begotten Son* (one in nature, one in Godship), *that whoever* (anyone) *believes in Him* (continue to believe) *shall not perish* (death) *but have everlasting* (salvation) *life"* (John 3:16-KJV).

I'm casting dispersion on those self-helps of gratification that you pick up or even your works in the organization we called today as "Church" for we are saved by faith through grace and not by works. (Ephesians 2:9: *"not of works, lest any man should boast."*) Just step away and hear the word of God as it speaks to your heart. Look at how many times you have attended seminars, conferences, or revivals. For that moment you are energized, for that second you feel the tormenting spirits have ceased their torture. But after the moment passes, you find you are still bound by the same compulsions, wants, and desires. The answer isn't in the works you do, the money you give, the retreats you attend, or how many times you confess at the altar. The message I am portraying is Jesus, and only Jesus is the grace that can save you. He is not a temporary fix but a permanent solution to all of your life's addictions.

Scripture states in Matthew 11:28-30. *"Come unto me, all ye that labour and are heavy laden, and I will give you rest. Take my yoke upon you and learn of me; for I am meek and lowly in heart: and ye shall find rest unto your souls. For my yoke is easy, and my burden is light."* The word yoke is from the Greek word "zygos" (pronounced zugos) which means: a) a yoke that is put on draught cattle; b) burden or bondage as that of slavery. In understanding the usage of this word let's look at the first definition (Resounding the Faith 2018). A yoke that is put on draught cattle is used to lead a pair of oxen and set the pace and direction. The lead ox would establish the pace for the other ox to follow; the reasoning for this is that the farmer hopes that the untrained or temperamental ox will learn from the lead so that they can labor together to accomplish a common task. Now let's examine the spiritual equivalent. In being yoked with Christ, we submit ourselves to His leading, His guidance, and Him. Being yoked with Christ allows Him to lead us, and we must submit all our power and ability to his leading. As we seek to walk with Him every day under His easy yoke, we will learn of Him, from Him, and by Him.

In seeking to walk with Him, we will learn who He is and become more and more like Him as we daily follow Him. This consistent walk with Christ is not a "today on, tomorrow off," or aa "hit-and-miss syndrome," but a walk of consistency that describes a mature and obedient life with Him. The inconsistent life that you are accustomed to living is one that characterizes most Christian believers today. When we daily walk with Christ, supping with Him as He sups with us, we take on His characteristics. We take on His attitudes, His reactions, His concerns, and His desires. We become more one or holy with Him and the Father. Learning of Christ will develop a life full of meekness and a humble heart; this meekness and humbly are not of our own but that of Him. Just as Christ, *"Though he were a Son, yet learned he obedience by the things which he suffered* (Heb. 5:8), we must learn obedience through the things that we suffer. We must submit to His leading so we may learn of Him and ultimately become Christ-centered.

Finally, now in an understanding of the action, let's look at the purpose of being yoked with Christ. As we continue to submit and commit our ways unto Christ, He will bring you into a life of labor and rest, for in this life we offer all of our strength and abilities to Him who from the beginning formed us in our mother's womb. Through resting in our labors, we receive the power and labor of Christ Jesus who is our hope of glory; it is no longer you that does this but Christ who lives within you. This empowerment is through the Holy Spirit of God and the labor we find is in His Spirit, therefore find rest in Him.

If these characteristics are true, then why is your lifestyle (lust of the flesh, the lust of the eyes, and pride of life) getting you into things that distract you and prevent you from feeing yourself from the addictions that have you bound? The Scripture speaks of how you can be made free from your bondage of sin and destruction. This begs the question, is it a spiritual discipline one lacks?

Chapter 17

My House

> *For we know that if our earthly house of this tabernacle were dissolved, we have a building of God, a house not made with hands, eternal in the heavens For in this we groan, earnestly desiring to be clothed upon with our house which is from heaven: If so be that being clothed we shall not be found naked.*
> *(*2 Corinthians 5:1-3, KJV)

The phrase "we know" in the first verse is translated from the Greek word "oidamen," meaning "to know intuitively" as a result of being a child of God. It is the knowledge that accompanies the new birth in Christ Jesus. The verse continues, "if our earthly house of this tabernacle [tent]," What Paul is saying here is that the spirit is the real person found in the body. This body is represented by the Greek word "skenon" (tent) which refers to the material portion of a person (Biblestudytools.com 2020). Paul continues to explain that though this earthly body ("house") will be "dissolved," God has promised there will be a "building of God" (Barcley 2020) This is a description of the death of the mortal body, yet it is intended to be an encouragement for the believer as he looks at death. The word that is translated as "building" is the Greek word "oikodomen," which means "the process of building something" (StudyLight.org 2020). The basic idea in this verse is that God is building a new house for the believer's spirit which will be disembodied at the point of death, leaving the body remaining on earth. This indicates that God will create something completely new. Then Paul uses the word "oikian" meaning "dwelling place," which refers to the completion of the eternal body (Biblehub.com 2020).

Two qualities of this new body must be understood. First, it will be similar to the present one and identifiable, yet not identical because it is not going to be made by human hands; it will be produced by God. The word translated as "not made with hands" is "acheiropoieton." This is the same word that the Lord used in Mark 14:58 when He spoke of destroying the temple, which was made by the hands of men, and in three days building another not made by man. Christ was speaking of His body following His resurrection. Although His own body was "made of a woman" at His birth (Gal. 4:4), no human being was involved at the time of His resurrection. The believer's human body will have the same outcome. The first time, when one is born into this world, the body is physically produced. However, at the resurrection by Christ of the righteous dead (1 Thess. 4:15-17), God will change them to new, glorified bodies (1 Cor. 15:50-57).

The second quality is the Greek word 'aionion' which means eternal (Slick 2020) This idea of eternalness focuses in on what characterizes God Himself. The life that is given at salvation to believers is the promise of eternal life (aionios, zoe), not denoting the duration of a period, but the quality of life. This life can never be lost or taken away once a person accepts Jesus Christ as Lord and Savior. "Aionios," however, is always related to time using the form "aion," speaking to "age or generation." One must consider its usage in 2 Corinthians 4:17-18 where contrast is made to *"the things which are seen.... are temporal"* and the affliction the Corinthians were undergoing to the *"more exceeding and eternal weight of glory."* Therefore, "aionios" means that which is not temporal, cannot be lost, nor destroyed. Paul gives the location of this *"life to be"* as *"in the heavens"* (see also 1 Cor. 8:5, 15:57; 2 Cor. 5:2,12:2). Paul recognized this place to be where God is and where the believer will find his ultimate rest (1 Thess. 4:17-18).

Forgiveness, Then Healing

One of the most prominent things in a Christian's life which hinders him from reaching the high calling of God is unforgiveness. Unforgiveness can harm our physical health and disrupt our mental being, but most of all, it will hinder our spiritual walk with God. In his letter to the Hebrews, Paul warns us about a root of bitterness: *"Looking diligently lest any man fail of the grace of God; lest any root of bitterness springing up trouble you, and thereby many be defiled"* (Heb. 12:15). When a root of bitterness is planted in our life, we can be assured unforgiveness is the fertilizer that makes it grow. As Paul warned, if we allow the root of bitterness in our life, we have failed the grace of God.

Another word for the root of bitterness is hard feelings. Hard feelings develop when we fail to forgive those who trespass against us. When we fail to forgive, it sets a whole chain of events in motion that eventually robs us of our peace. It causes us to become resentful, and then the basest of emotions take over; we seek to get even with those who have hurt us.

A bitter root in our life always produces bitter fruit, until everything we think or do seems wrong and we become discontent with ourselves and those around us. Paul knew and understood how important it was to have contentment in his life: *"Not that I speak in respect of want: for I have learned, in whatsoever state I am, therewith to be content"* (Phil. 4:11).

Today we live in a violent world where people never seem to have enough. Their lives are in constant turmoil because of wanting and desiring everything they see. These people will do anything to fulfill their wants and desires. Their discontentment keeps the police busy, the doctors' offices booked, and the criminal and divorce court dockets filled. They forget the words of Paul to Timothy: *"But godliness with contentment is great gain"* (1 Timothy 6:6).

So how do we gain contentment with our God and with each other? First, we must bridle our wants and desires, then secondly, we must produce forgiveness in every aspect of our life. John the Beloved wrote, *"Whosoever sins ye remit, they are remitted unto them, and whosoever sins ye retain, they are retained"* (John 20:23).

Unforgiveness is a sin. The word remit means "to send away or forgive." When we forgive those who sin against us, then we are free of the sin of unforgiveness. But if we do not forgive, then we retain or hold on to the sin; we are stuck with it, and it does its damaging work. Unforgiveness gives a place for the root of bitterness and begins a downward plunge in our Spiritual walk. It will affect all our relationships.

We must forgive. The universe operates according to God's well-crafted design, and human relationships are no exception. For us to live the abundant life as the Word of God promises us, and to experience healing and release from devastating relationships and circumstances, we must practice the principle of forgiveness.

Forgiveness must be automatic in a Christian's life. The act must be practiced until it becomes perfected in our life. The Lord Jesus gives us many reasons to forgive in His Word: *"For if ye forgive men their trespasses, your heavenly Father will also forgive you: But if ye forgive not men their trespasses, neither will your heavenly Father forgive your trespasses"* (Matt. 6:14-15).

Those who do not forgive are not forgiven of the Father. Therefore, they remain in their sin and they have no hope in God until they forgive. They harbor hurts, devolving deeper and deeper in their unforgiveness until their whole thought processes are consumed with these ungodly, disrupting thoughts. The prophet Isaiah gives us insight as to how we can be pleasing to God: *"Thou wilt keep him in perfect peace, whose mind is stayed on Thee: because he trusteth in Thee"* (Isa. 26:3).

We cannot have the promised, perfect peace when our minds are on the hurts others have caused us. And as Matthew warned, we cannot have our sins forgiven if we have not forgiven others who have sinned against us. If we are serious about our relationship with our God, then it becomes imperative to forgive, forgive, and forgive. Even the early disciples had a problem understanding the importance of forgiveness: *"Then came Peter to Him, and said, Lord, how oft shall my brother sin against me, and I forgive him? Seven times? Jesus saith unto him, I say not unto thee, Until seven times: but, Until seventy times seven"* (Matt. 18:21-22).

Peter was the inquisitive one, but his heart was to be pleasing in the sight of God. Jesus's answer has stunned people down through the ages. Sometimes seven times seems like a lot, but Jesus said we are to forgive 490 times. Jesus must have known that after we forgive 490 times, then forgiveness would become part of our being. Jesus also knew that 490 was the number of spiritual perfection (7 is God's perfect number, and 10 is the number of completion; so 7 times 7 times 10 represents spiritual perfection). When we come into spiritual perfection, we will not hold grudges, we will not harbor hard feelings toward others, and we will be free to enter into God's perfect peace because our minds will have stayed on Him.

Jesus understood the power of forgiveness. He related the story of a man who owed his master a large sum of money. The man asked his master to forgive his debt, and the master forgave the whole debt.

But the same servant went out, and found one of his fellow servants, which owed him an hundred pence: and he laid hands on him, and took him by the throat, saying, Pay me that thou owest. And his fellow servant fell down at his feet, and besought him, saying, Have patience with me, and I will pay thee all. And he would not: but went and cast him into prison, till he should pay the debt. So when his fellow servants saw what was done, they were very sorry, and came and told unto their lord all that was done. Then his lord, after that he had called him, said unto him, O thou wicked servant, I forgave thee all that debt, because thou desiredst me: Shouldest not thou also have had compassion on thy fellow servant, even as I had pity on Thee? And his lord was wroth, and delivered him to the tormentors, till he should pay all that was due unto him. Matthew 18:28-34

Many times, we are like the ungrateful servant. We want God to forgive all our sins and bless us, but do we forgive others who have sinned against us. If we are like the ungrateful servant, what can we expect? Jesus tells us, *"And his lord was wroth, and delivered him to the tormentors, till he should pay all that was due unto him. So likewise shall My heavenly Father do also unto you, if ye from your hearts forgive not every one Her brother their trespasses"* (Matt. 18:34-35). The ungrateful servant was delivered to the tormentors. Then Jesus made us the promise, *"If we do not forgive every one of our brother's trespasses, so our heavenly Father will do to you"*(Matt 18:35). Do we wonder why some of God's people are suffering? They need to look at their lives to see if there is unforgiveness that has not been dealt with.

If we do not forgive, what kind of prison are we in? We are held captive in the prison of our minds. It is a prison of unseen bars and unopened locks, and we will be held there until we practice the act of unforgiveness. Forgiveness is the only key that can open those prison doors and set us free. The prison not only keeps us in but locks others out.

There are two aspects of forgiveness: one is the act of forgiving, the other is the act of forgetting. Have you ever had a genuine desire to forgive a person and have said all the right words—"I forgive so and so for whatever the offense against me was?— only to discover moments, days, or weeks later that you were carrying on an argument with them in your mind?

You may think you have forgiven them, but have you truly forgotten their trespass against you? If the trespass is still in your heart and mind, then you have not truly forgiven them. A good test of whether or not you have genuinely forgiven a person from the heart is that when you think of them, you do not negative thoughts or reactions. Jesus gave us insight when He said we must forgive from the heart. If we still have negative thoughts against a person, then our heart has not changed toward that person and we still suffer from unforgiveness. Until we forgive and truly forget, our whole nature becomes one of getting even with our mouth and/or with our actions, even as far as wishing for that person's death. Jesus spoke many times about forgiveness because He knew the devastating effect unforgiveness has on our body. After all, He created us and knows our very being. *"Judge not, and ye shall not be judged: condemn not, and ye shall not be condemned: forgive, and ye shall be forgiven"* (Luke 6:37). If we judge others, then God will judge us. If we condemn others, then God will cause condemnation to come upon us. If we do not forgive, then we have no forgiveness for the sins we commit against God or His people.

Unforgiveness leads to judging and condemning others, but when we forgive, we set in motion God's forgiving grace in our lives. Then, and only then, will we be set free from the prison-house that held us in bondage. Paul knew the power of forgiveness: *"And be ye kind one to another, tenderhearted, forgiving one another, even as God for Christ's sake hath forgiven you"* (Eph. 4:32).

When we are kind and tenderhearted to one another, forgiving one another. and living in harmony with one another, then we truly prove to God that we deserve His forgiveness toward us. When we do not forgive, we tie God's hands so He cannot forgive us. John the Beloved wrote, *"If we confess our sins, He is faithful and just to forgive us our sins, and to cleanse us from all unrighteousness"* (1 John 1:9). When we confess our sins, then God will not only forgive our sins but confessing our sin will cleanse us from all unrighteousness.

Unforgiveness is nothing new. It began in the Garden of Eden. Cain was unable to forgive his brother, Abel because Abel's sacrifice was acceptable before God and he was not. That led to the first murder. How many metaphorical murders have there been in your life because of unforgiveness? Unforgiveness leads to hatred. Hatred in our bodies is like a festering sore; the more you pick at it, the worse it becomes until it consumes our entire attention.

King David committed more sins than we could ever be guilty of, but David had a repentant heart. Many of David's psalms were psalms of repentance. Take Psalm 51:3-4 for example: *"For I acknowledge my transgressions: and my sin is ever before me. Against thee, thee only, have I sinned, and done this evil in Thy sight: that Thou mightest be justified when Thou speakest, and be clear when Thou judgest."* David knew when he sinned it was against God. Anytime we break one of God's royal laws, our sin is against our God. David's tender heart convicted him of his sin.

Every person born is born with a conscience. Our conscience is what convicts us of our sin. In his letter to Timothy, Paul warns the people, *"Now the Spirit speaketh expressly, that in the latter times some shall depart from the faith, giving heed to seducing spirits, and doctrines of devils; Speaking lies in hypocrisy; having their conscience seared with a hot iron"* (1I Timothy 4:1-2). The Spirit revealed to Paul, *" in the latter times some will depart from the faith"* (1 Tim. 4:1a). This is evident today. Many give heed to seducing spirits and the doctrines of devils. The Muslims are a perfect example of these doctrines of devils. They speak lies in hypocrisy, wearing a costume of Christianity, simply acting out a lie. As Paul reveals, they'll have their consciences seared or hardened with a hot iron. God can no longer convict these of their sin therefore they do not repent, and they remain in their sin condition, judging others as they remaining in their unrighteousness. Although David committed many sins toward God, he remained tenderhearted, always repenting, and seeking God's forgiveness. It was said of David, he was a man after God's own heart. David's whole desire, as ours should be, was to stand before God clean and whole.

Jesus revealed to John on the isle of Patmos. *"And before the throne there was a sea of glass like unto crystal"* (Rev. 4:6). The sea of glass is God's creation who will stand before Him on the Day of Judgment. God knows our innermost being. We can hide nothing from Him, so we might just as well confess our sin so we can be healed and made whole.

The all-wise Solomon shared his wisdom when he wrote, *"He that covereth his sins shall not prosper: but whoso confesseth and forsaketh them shall have mercy"* (Prov. 28:13). If we want God's mercy in our life, then we must confess and forsake our sins. Only then can we obtain God's mercy. If we try to cover (hide) our sin, we will never prosper in the things of God.

Our sin is not only the sin of unforgiveness and hard feelings, but it includes our continual grievance toward our brothers and sisters. Until we deal with these in our life, we cannot expect to obtain God's mercy. David, who understood God's mercy and forgiveness probably more than any man, proclaimed of God's mercy, *"Who forgiveth all thine iniquities; who healeth all thy diseases"* (Ps. 103:3).

David knew how the sin of unforgiveness affects man's physical being. Many are sick in their bodies because they are bound up in hate and unforgiveness. They suffer depression and become bitter until their lives become a festering mess. They are miserable and try to make all those around them miserable. They continue in their miserable state until their whole body, soul, and spirit are devastated. They wonder why they no longer enjoy God's mercy and forgiveness in their life. James writes, *"Grudge not one against another, brethren, lest ye be condemned: behold, the judge standeth before the door"* (James 5:9). The word grudge means "to groan with grief." We are not to grudge or hold grudges against anyone, or we will be condemned. The Judge truly stands at the door to judge those who hold grudges. A grudge is simply unforgiveness.

Peter gives us further insight as to what God expects of us: *"Use hospitality one to another without grudging"* (1 Pet. 4:9). The word grudging used in the Scripture is different from today and means "to murmur and complain " (Collins English Dictionary 2020). We are to show hospitality to one another, even to those we do not like, without murmuring or complaining.

Three men in God's Word showed perfect forgiveness. The first was Joseph, who was sold into slavery by his brothers, falsely accused by Potipher's wife, and forgotten by Pharaoh's butler. Yet when he became the second ruler in Egypt, he got even with none of these individuals. He told his brothers that God did all that had been done to preserve life. Joseph not only forgave from his mouth, but he also forgave from his heart.

We are not made aware of how God is using us in any situation He puts us in. Jesus is our perfect example of forgiveness. When He was beaten unmercifully and nailed to the cross, He could still say, *"Father, forgive them"* (Luke 23:34).

Certainly, Stephen is an example to us of forgiveness. Even as he was being stoned, he too forgave those throwing the rocks. Once we decide, depend, and obey, we will be able to:

1) Forgive others who trespass against us.

2) Receive forgiveness from others who have trespassed against us.

3) Forgive ourselves

The Bible explains in great detail what happens to a saint when they harbor bitterness, resentment, and unforgiveness. Matthew 18:23-35 tells us that if we do not forgive people, it will consume and destroy us. What does hateful thoughts toward another who has harmed, hurt, and disappointed do to us? Allow me to deal with the natural man with light spiritual concepts.

When you forgive, you are helping yourself more than the other person. Many people look at forgiving people who have hurt them as being hard to do. To me, it seemed so unfair for others to receive forgiveness when I was the one who received the pain and hurt. I thought they received their freedom without having to pay for the pain they caused. But then I realized I am in the way, trying to get revenge, holding onto ill-feelings, or taking care of the situation myself instead of allowing God, then that tells God He has no obligation to deal with that person. This is directly against his will, especially since He told us "Vengeance is mine.". The act of forgiving is our seed of obedience to God's word. Once we've sown our seed, He is faithful to bring a harvest of blessing to us one way or another.

Another way that forgiveness helps you is that it releases God to do His work in you. You become happier and feel better physically when you are not filled with the poison of unforgiveness. Serious diseases can develop as a result of the stress and pressure that bitterness, resentment, and unforgiveness put on a person. In Mark 11:22-26, he teaches us that unforgiveness hinders our faith from working. The Father can't forgive your sins if you don't forgive others. We reap what we sow. Sow mercy and you'll reap mercy, sow judgment and you'll reap judgment. So do yourself a favor and forgive.

There are still more benefits to forgiveness. Your fellowship with God flows more freely when you're willing to forgive, but it is blocked by unforgiveness. Forgiveness also keeps Satan from gaining an advantage over us (2 Cor. 2:10-11). Ephesians 4:26-27 tells us not to let the sun go down on our wrath or give the devil any such foothold in our life. Remember, the devil must have a foothold before he can get a stronghold. Do not provide a way for Satan to torture you. Be quick to forgive.

Brothers and sisters, how can you despise one person but love another? It becomes difficult to treat anybody right when your heart isn't right. Even people you want to love may be suffering from your bitterness, resentment, and unforgiveness. How is it affecting your children, extended family, coworkers, and acquaintances? Therefore, the question is, "How do I forgive when I am hurting so badly"?

The first thing is to DECIDE. You will never forgive yourself or anyone else if you wait until you feel like it. Choose today to obey God and steadfastly resist the devil in his attempts to poison you with bitter thoughts, confused emotions, and angry resentment. If you decide to today that enough is enough, and you will be obedient to God concerning forgiveness, then God will heal your wounded emotions in due season (read Matthew 6:12-14).

The second thing you need to do is DEPEND. Depending on God, however, cannot be done without the power of the Holy Spirit. It's too hard to do on your own. If you are truly willing, God will enable you, but you must humble yourself and cry out to Him for help. This is not a good-feeling situation; this is a trust and depends on the situation. In John 20:22-23, Jesus breathed on the disciples and said, *"Receive the Holy Spirit!"* His next instruction was about forgiving people. Ask God to breathe the Holy Spirit on you so you can forgive those who've hurt you.

Third, OBEY. The Word tells us several things we're to do concerning forgiving our enemies. This is to pray for your enemies and those who abuse and misuse you as well as pray for their happiness and welfare (Luke 6:26-28). As you pray, God can give those who have wronged you the revelation that will bring them out of deception. They may not even be aware they hurt you, or maybe they're aware but are so self-centered that they don't care. Either way, they need revelation.

Bless and do not curse them (Rom. 12:14). In the Greek, "to bless" means "to speak well of: and "to curse" means "to speak evil of." You can't walk in forgiveness and be a gossip. You must stop repeating the offense. You can't get over it if you continue to talk about it. Proverbs 17:9 says that he who covers an offense seeks love.

When it comes to forgiving those who have hurt you, yes, it is hard, and, yes, you must deny yourself and be obedient to the Word of God. Forgive quickly. The quicker you do it, the easier it is. Forgive freely. Matthew 10:8 NKJV says, *"Freely you have received, freely give."* Forgive means "to excuse a fault, absolve from payment, pardon, send away, cancel, and bestow favor unconditionally" (Dictionary.com 2020). When you forgive, you must cancel the debt. Do not spend your life paying and collecting debts. Hebrews 10:30 says God repays and settles the cases of His people. Let God restore you from you, for past injustices. Do not try to collect from the people who hurt you because the people who hurt you can't pay you.

Also, forgive yourself for past sins and hurts you have caused others. You can't pay people back, so ask God to deliver you and help you forgive those who despitefully misused you. Remember, *"vengeance is mind saith the Lord, I will repay"* (Romans 12:19). God is always just. There may be things you don't understand, but God loves you, and people make a serious mistake when they don't receive help from the only One who can truly help them.

You even need to forgive all circumstances, named and unnamed. No matter what and who it may be, get rid of all poison that comes from bitterness, resentment, and unforgiveness. And remember Proverbs 4:23: *"Keep and guard your heart with all vigilance…for out of it flow the springs of life."* Point-blank, unforgiveness is spiritual filthiness, so allow God's Word to wash you thoroughly.

Forgiving ourselves is the most important aspect of all three steps I have shared. Many err in God's Word. They get a "woe is me attitude" until they convince themselves they are only failures and cannot succeed in God. Many continue in this attitude for the rest of their lives. God wants us to know that if we ask Him, He will forgive us. Our brothers and sisters want us to know, if we ask them, they, too, will forgive us. But the most important forgiveness is when we forgive ourselves for our past failures. When we practice the art of forgiveness, then God's grace and mercy will abound in our life. Swallow the pride, deal with the hurts, and be set free to live the abundant life God has promised you.

Chapter 18

Judging—Who Me?

This chapter is not intended to point the finger or to judge you, but to bring you into an awareness of your flesh and its working members with the world and Satan. The word judge is used in such a negative sense in our society because it carries a connotation that you are being a hypocrite. So what does the word mean, *"Judge (to distinguish; i.e. decide [mentally or judicially]) not according to the appearance, but judge righteous (God's law) judgment (decision)"* (John 7:24).

In being a Christian, we have to understand and practice professing true Christianity. A good portion of the world's population hasn't professed Christ as their Lord and Savior because they have not been exposed to the Gospel of Jesus Christ. And those that have confessed have not been sincere in their walk with Christ. Is it a matter of sincerity or a matter of just being a part of a sect, group, and/or organization? It is not a matter of sincerity or following the majority, it is a matter of finding the genuine truth regarding the purpose of human existence and the way to fulfill the awesome purpose that God has in store for you.

Therefore, I ask, is being sincere religiosity enough? No! All religions are not based on equality. If you are willing to prove to yourself that the one great Creator is the true God and that the

Bible is His inspired revelation to mankind, then you must understand there is only one way to eternal life and that through Jesus Christ. That means, not your grandma or grandpa's Christianity or anyone else's, but that solely modeled by Jesus the Christ. Apostle Peter stated:

> *Be it known unto you all, and to all the people of Israel, that by the name of Jesus Christ of Nazareth, whom ye crucified, whom God raised from the dead, even by him doth this man stand here before you whole. This is the stone which was set at naught of you builders, which is become the head of the corner. Neither is there salvation in any other: for there is none other name under heaven given among men, whereby we must be saved."* Acts 4:10-12

Moreover, very few professing Christians comprehend the enormity of the deception orchestrated by Satan. Some find it hard to grasp the fact that Satan has not only deceived those in the pagan, non-Christian world, but he has devised a counterfeit Christianity that has mesmerized millions who sincerely think they are following the Christ of the Bible. Like the apostle, Paul warned the Corinthians, *"But I fear, lest by any means, as the serpent beguiled (to speak or live by treachery, deceived) Eve through his subtlety (craftiness), so your minds should be corrupted from the simplicity that is in Christ. For if he that cometh preacheth another Jesus, whom we have not preached, or if ye receive another spirit, which ye have not received, or another gospel, which ye have not accepted, ye might well bear with him"* (2 Cor. 11:3-4).

That's right, a counterfeit Christianity that moves within your flesh. This religion does not require you to give up or change anything you have or are doing in your life. Such false Christianity encourages you to continue to live in the lust of the flesh, the lust of the eyes, and the pride of life. Within this counterfeit Christianity, there are similarities to true Christianity that often are unnoticed by the naked eye, just like a counterfeit dollar looks like the real thing but isn't. So it is with Satan, the master deceiver.

To fool oneself in thinking that Satan is not real is his first deception to Christians. Satan is the invisible god of this world for he is the deceiver of men and nations (2 Cor. 4:4). Satan hasn't changed his tactics in beguiling mankind and continuing as he did in Jesus's time. Jesus himself condemned the religious leaders of His day for their hypocrisy. Those ecclesiastical figures made a pretense of being godly yet refused to follow the spiritual intent of God's law, *"having a form of godliness, but denying the power thereof; form such turn away"* (2 Tim. 4:5). Jesus attributed to them Satan's character, using the analogy that since their father was Satan, they could only behave like their father as a son does. *"Ye are of your father the devil, and the lusts of your father ye will do. He was a murderer from the beginning, and abode not in the truth, because there is no truth in him. When he speaketh a lie, he speaketh of his own: for he is a liar, and the father of it"* (John 8:44).

The apostle Paul warns Christians about the great deception caused by Satan and his ministers:

> *For such are false apostles, deceitful workers, transforming themselves into the apostles of Christ. And no marvel; for Satan himself is transformed into an angel of light. Therefore, it is no great thing if his ministers also be transformed as the ministers of righteousness; whose end shall be according to their works.* 2 Corinthians 11:13-15.

Therefore, we have to be sure of what we allow our members to partake of and be party too. Because Satan's ministers are working in deception to increase the kingdom of this devil in this last day. Even though satan's minister may look and sound like a servant of God, they preach another Jesus and proclaim a different gospel than that of the Jesus of the Bible. Therefore, it is up to each individual to thoroughly study the Bible and to prove what Jesus and the early apostles taught. Merely listening to a sermon does not the completed task; it is taking what you have heard Study, study, and study the unadulterated Word of God. You must open the Bible to know what He is saying to you.

You may not understand the Word of God, but I suggest you follow this little method. First, *"But seek ye first the kingdom of God, and his righteousness: and all these things shall be added unto you"* (Matt.6:33).

Secondly,

> Have faith in God. *For verily I say unto you, That whosoever shall say unto this mountain, Be thou removed, and be thou cast into the sea; and shall not doubt in his heart, but shall believe that those things which he saith shall come to pass; he shall have whatsoever he saith. Therefore I say unto you, What things soever ye desire, when ye **pray**, **believe** that ye **receive** the, and ye shall have them."* (Mark 11:22-24).

Thirdly, the Jesus said, ASK; A = Ask, S = Seek, K = knock: *"Ask, and it shall be given you; seek, and ye shall find; knock, and it shall be opened unto you; For every one that asketh receiveth; and he that seeketh findeth; and to him that knocketh it shall be opened"* (Matt. 7:7-8). And finally, Timothy offers the last step: *"Study to show thyself approved unto God, a workman that needeth not to be ashamed, rightly dividing (dissect) the word of truth.* (2 Tim. 2:15). If we pick up our Bibles daily to read of the Jesus of the Bible and His characteristics, we will not find ourselves running after and being a part of unimportant church work (things we use to substitute our time with God) that has no bearing on salvation and the ways of Christ.

In understanding Satan's counterfeit Christianity, you must understand who the deceiver is and what his purpose is for you. Satan has only one purpose, and that is to keep you from entering the straight and narrow way. *"Enter ye in at the strait gate: for wide is the gate, broad is the way, that leadeth to destruction; and many there be which go in there at: Because strait is the gate, and narrow is the way which leadeth unto life, and few there be that find it"* (Matt. 7:13-14). He cannot physically stop you, however, he imparts his thoughts and we, within our flesh, carry out his pernicious ways. For example, if you have thought of slapping or hitting someone in anger, you have a choice: 1) To partake in that deed, or 2) To walk away or disdain the thought. That is how simple living the life of Christ is. All you need is to ask yourself, "Do I live for Him or do I live for myself." We make decisions every day whether we chose to be a part of something or not. Why not make a conscientious thought to do the will of God, read His Word, study what He has in store for you?

How can you learn to love if you do not know what love is? How do you live free from sin if you have never believed that you can? All these things and much more are in the Word of God and the word of God is Jesus, the hope of glory. Scripture states it like this:

> *"In the beginning was the Word, and the Word was with God, and the Word was God. The same was in the beginning with God. All things were made by him; and*

without him was not any thing made that was made. In him was life; and the life was the light (illuminator) of men" (John 1:1-4).

Counterfeit Christianity extenuates every part of the lust and its workings which is the manifestation of the action of our flesh. In many churches today, there is a mixture of this counterfeit Christianity within the confounds of the body of Christ. We can see practices today are not the same as the early, true church recorded in the New Testament. Do you know it is vital to know whether there has been purposeful mixing of false pagan practices and rituals with the true teachings of Christ, the apostles, and the Bible? "Many historians, such as Edward Gibbon, have noted the change brought about by great numbers of pagans flocking into the early "Christian church and mixing their pagan customs and beliefs with those of the church" (Gibbon & Trevor-Roper 2000). You can see evidence of this today of how some churches have sprung from the same root as paganism.

Satan has created an entire system of counterfeit programs, Bible studies, worship halls, prayer breakfasts, musicals, and more. He has cleverly guided vain religious leaders to introduce completely pagan ideas and practices into "Christianity.". Many people blindly assume since the word "Christianity" is stamped on the outside of the package that the religion of Jesus Christ is being offered. Little do they know that false concepts of God, of Jesus Christ and His message, of the purpose and way of eternal life, have been wrapped up in a lovely, crystal package largely called "Christianity." But I want you to know this is delivery of such counterfeit-Christianity is from the anti-Christ, Satan.

This corrupted Christianity has captured most of mankind, whether saved or unsaved and has cost many from receiving the true God. Within this deception, mankind has become confused and inept to the point of concern.

> *This know also, that in the last days perilous times shall come. For men shall be lovers of their ownselves, covetous, boasters, proud, blasphemers, disobedient to parents, unthankful, unholy, Without natural affection, trucebreakers, false accusers, incontinent, fierce, despisers of those that are good, Traitors, heady, high minded, lovers of pleasures more than lovers of God; Having a form of godliness, but denying the power thereof: from such turn away. For of this sort are they which creep into houses, and lead captive silly women laden with sins, led away with divers lusts, Ever learning, and never able to come to the knowledge of the truth."* 2 Timothy 3:1-7)

The Bible tells us: *"Prove all things; holdfast that which is good"* (1 Thess. 5:21). In this verse, the great Apostle Paul is exhorting us as a community of believers to act in discerning what is truth and what is false to distinguish what is true or false revelation before holding fast what is fact Historian after historian acknowledges that the original Christianity of Jesus and the apostles were dramatically changed within a few centuries after Jesus's death. As noted, historian Will Durant wrote:

> Christianity did not destroy paganism; it adopted it. The Greek mind, dying, came to a transmigrated life in the theology and liturgy of the Church; the Greek language, having reigned for centuries over philosophy, became the vehicle of Christian literature and ritual; the Greek mysteries passed down into the impressive

mystery of the Mass. Other pagan cultures contributed to the syncretistic result. From Egypt came the ideas of a divine trinity...and a personal immortality of reward and punishment; from Egypt the adoration of the Mother and Child, and the mystic theosophy that made Neoplatonism and Gnosticism, and obscured the Christian creed: there, too, Christian monasticism would find its exemplars and its source. From Phrygia came the worship of the Great Mother; from Syria the resurrection drama of Adonis; from Thrace, perhaps, the cult of Dionysus, the dying and saving good.... The Mithraic ritual so closely resembled the Eucharistic sacrifice of the Mass that Christian fathers charged the Devil with inventing these similarities to mislead frail minds. Christianity was the last great creation of the ancient pagan world...[The Eucharist] was a conception long sanctified by time; the pagan mind needed no schooling to receive it; by embodying the 'mystery of the Mass,' Christianity became the last and greatest of the mystery religions. (Durant 1953, 599).

And there is Paul Johnson, who is one of many highly respected historians, who openly acknowledges that the biblical seventh-day Sabbath observed by Christ and the original apostles was changed.

"Many Christians did not make a clear distinction between this sun-cult and their own. They referred to Christ 'driving his chariot across the sky,' they held their services on Sunday, knelt towards the East and had their nativity-feast on 25 December, the birthday of the sun at the winter solstice. During the later pagan revival under the Emperor Julian, many Christians found it easy to apostatize because of this confusion; the Bishop of Troy told Julian he had always prayed secretly to the sun. Constantine never abandoned sun-worship and kept the sun on his coins. He made Sunday into a day of rest." (Johnson 2008, 67-69)

Also, mainstream religious author Jesse Lyman Hurlbut explains:

> The forms and ceremonies of paganism gradually crept into the worship. Some of the old heathen feasts became church festivals with change of name and of worship. About 405$_{AD}$ images of saints and martyrs began to appear in the churches, at first as memorials, then in succession revered, adored, and worshiped. The adoration of the Virgin Mary was substituted for the worship of Venus and Diana; the Lord's Supper became a sacrifice in place of a memorial; and the elder evolved from a preacher into a priest…The church and the state became one when Christianity was adopted as the religion of the empire, and out of the unnatural union arose two evils, one in the eastern, the other in the western provinces. In the east the state dominated the church until it lost all energy and uplifting life. In the west ["Rome," Ed.] as we shall see, the church gradually usurped power over the state, and the result was not Christianity but a more or less corrupt hierarchy controlling the nations of Europe, making the church mainly a political machine. (Hurlbut 1930, 79-80)

Incorporation of paganistic beliefs, like in the early church, continues today. Congregants, pastors, ministers, prophets, evangelist, and others use a created Christianity as a cloak of mischievousness. For example: *"Now as Jannes and Jambres withstood Moses, so do these also resist the truth: men of corrupt minds, reprobate concerning the faith"* (2 Tim. 3:1:8).

In knowing this truth, where do we go from here? Each of us needs to follow what Apostle Paul instructed *"Examine yourselves, whether ye be in the faith; prove your own selves. Know ye not your own selves, how that Jesus Christ is in you, except ye be reprobates (unapproved, i.e.: rejected; by implying worthless (literal or morally):–castaway, rejected, reprobate.)?"* (2 Cor. 13:5).

We must be able to recognize who and what spirit is always working within us; we must be able to recognize what is of God and what is counterfeit Christianity. The documented historical information presented in this chapter is not just a philosophical viewpoint or argument against genuinely pagan practices, but rather an eye-opener to one of Satan's strongest devices, and that is deception. It would be ashamed to continue to go in err thinking that we are in truth to hear the Lord say, *"Not everyone that saith unto me, Lord, Lord, shall enter into the kingdom of heaven; but he that doeth the will of my Father which is in heaven. Many will say to me in that day, Lord, Lord, have we not prophesied in thy name? and in thy name have cast out devils? And in thy name done many wonderful works? And then will I profess unto them, I never knew you: depart from me, ye that work iniquity"* (Matt. 7:21-23).

Satan can only whisper to us the deeds of the flesh, however, when we partake of his words and taste of his desires, then we sup with him in a manner that brings forth death if we continue. The apostle Paul states it this way: *"Know ye not, that to whom ye yield yourselves servants to obey, his servants ye are to whom ye obey; whether of sin unto death, or of obedience unto righteousness?"* (Rom. 6:16). Therefore, if we yield our bodies, minds, and souls unto the gratification of the flesh and its lust. then we are a servant to it. Becoming a slave to the addictions of the flesh, no matter what they are, is also how Satan deceives mankind into thinking this is alright. God loves the individual but not the continuous act of sin that we do in our flesh. It brings me back to this statement—as long as we continue to partake of this sinful nature which is our flesh, working hand in hand with Satan and his counterfeit-Christianity, we will not have any part of the kingdom of God.

Chapter 19

COUNTERFEIT RELIGION: THE CHANGING TIMES AND LAWS

The prophet Daniel speaks of a *"little horn"* (Dan. 7:8) which *"shall speak great words against the Most High…and think to change times and laws"* (Dan. 7:25) This little horn is a great religious authority that attempts to superimpose its view of dates and celebrations on an unsuspecting world in place of God's plan and instruction.

The Hebrew word translated "change" means to "transform, alter or set." The word translated "times" means "appointed occasions, seasons, or times." The Hebrew word translated "laws" means "decrees or laws of God." When putting together these words, the resulting phrase refers to an authority that attempts to "transform appointed occasions and seasons within the Law of God." Certainly, Christmas is a great example of how this has been done. God's instructions have been replaced with the religious traditions of men. The following quote reveals how this has happened. It also comes from the Encyclopedia Britannica under "Christianity":

Thus, the Easter liturgy has been developed more highly in the Eastern Orthodox Church and the Christmas liturgy more highly in the Roman Catholic Church...The Christian calendar is the most widely disseminated Christian institution. The seven-day week and the rhythm of the Christian festivals have been accepted even by most of the non-Christian countries. Despite energetic attempts at the introduction of a sliding work week, the seven-day week with work-free Sunday could not be eliminated even in Communist states with an Atheist world view. Even in Atheistic circles and organizations throughout the world, Christian holidays enjoy an undisputed popularity as work-free days... especially Christmas (Encyclopedia Britannica 2020).

It has been the ecclesiastical politicians referred to earlier who have sought to impose the modern "Christian" calendar on an unknowing world. It is these leaders who have *"And he shall speak great words against the most High, and shall wear out the saints of the Most High, and think to change times and laws: and they shall be given into his hand until a time and times and the dividing of time* (Daniel 7:25).

The Dangerous Power of Lies

One of Satan's names is Destroyer (Rev. 9:11). Nimrod, Saturn, Molech, and Baal, like Satan, are the fire gods who destroy and devour little children.

The real Jesus Christ was never in and never will be at Christmas. He cannot be put back into where He has never been. But the *"god of this world,"* Satan (2 Cor. 4:4), has always been at

Christmas. He is its author. The "Jesus" who is the focus of these seasons is NOT the true Jesus Christ of the Bible

Our true God commands that we *"must worship Him in spirit and truth"* (John 4:23-24). This does not mesh with the great Christmas and Santa Claus lies that all children so willingly believe. First Timothy 4:2 warns of those *"speaking lies in hypocrisy; having their conscience seared with a hot iron."* Parents can "burn" their children, to the point of searing them, with the Christmas deception and lie.

There is no safety in numbers in this world for those who keep Christmas because Satan, who is called *"the father of lies"* and *"a murderer from the beginning"* (John 8:44), has *"deceived the whole world"* (Rev.12:9). Turn to this verse and read it. Then recognize that Christmas is certainly a testimony to that great deception.

Christ refers to His Church as a *"little flock"* (Luke 12:32). Many other scripture verses show this. This Church does not have the large numbers of the respected, established brands of the Christianity of this world.

Another Jesus

Most have been taught that there is only one Jesus Christ. But God's Word speaks of a counterfeit, and this substitute Christ is identifiable in history. The proof? The apostle Paul warned of "another Jesus."

First, consider Paul's entire introduction as he sets the stage for the warning that follows: *"But I fear, lest by any means, as the serpent [Satan] beguiled Eve through his subtilty, so your minds should be corrupted from the simplicity that is in Christ"* (2 Cor. 11:3). Next consider the actual warning in the next verse: *"For if he that comes preaches ANOTHER JESUS, whom we have not preached, or if you receive another* spirit, *which you have not received, or another gospel, which you have not accepted, you might well bear with him"* (2 Cor. 11:4). The Corinthians seemed to bear with this without much resistance.

Paul, under the inspiration of the true Jesus Christ of the Bible, was moved to record the peril of unwittingly following "another Jesus.". Most have probably never considered the idea of a false Jesus—that there is such a thing as a wrong, different, or *"false Christ"* (Matt. 24:23-24) called "another Jesus." In the past, this "Jesus" corrupted the thinking of true Christians. This much is plain. But the subtilty of how this can happen, and how it has occurred in history, is so deceptive—so seductive—that even true Christians can unknowingly slip into worshipping this so-called Jesus. This is what was happening to the Corinthians.

People can worship in ways that represent things that are far different than what they sincerely believe. Bible "believers" today can think that they are worshipping the true Savior when they are worshipping a false savior—ANOTHER JESUS. The entirety of traditional Christianity is worshipping Nimrod, Saturn, Molech, and Baal. The modern mother/child "Mary/Jesus" emphasis, including the worshipful adoration of Mary by millions, is parallel with Nimrod and his mother, Semiramis, that cannot be missed (Semiramis invented polytheism and, with it, goddess worship).

Here is the point: many speak of "putting Christ back into Christmas," making Easter the "resurrection Sunday," adding Him back into what are other pagan customs. This is heard every year from thousands of pulpits and elsewhere. But the true Christ was never there. Just as a person cannot go back into their mother's womb or a room that he had never entered, Jesus Christ cannot be "put back" into an event that He has never been in, and that He hates. (see Mark 7:7.)

The Jesus that these preachers and religionists have in mind is another Christ, one with another gospel, and a different doctrine and teaching.

Chapter 20

WHAT SHOULD I DO?

As we draw to the end of this book, let's examine what God told His people they should do and the way they ought to teach their children.

Recall Jeremiah 7:31, where God condemned Israel for burning their children in the Valley of Tophet. Eight verses earlier (vs. 23-24), God made plain what He requires: *"But this thing commanded I them, saying, Obey My voice, and I will be your God, and you shall be My people: and walk you in all the ways that I have commanded you, that it may be well unto you. But they hearkened not…but walked…in the imagination of their evil heart."*

Human beings do not want to obey God (Rom. 8:7). They would rather follow their imagination. They do not understand that God wants their lives to go well;" He wants happiness, joy, and blessings to flow into people's lives. All these are the results of obeying Him.

God inspired Moses to warn parents of the grave responsibility they have in what and how they teach their children. Notice His instruction in Deuteronomy chapter 6, verses 1, 6-7, 20-21, and 25:

> *Now these are the commandments…which the* LORD *your God commanded to teach you, that you might do*

them in the land where you go to possess it...And these words, which I command you this day, shall be in your heart: And you shall teach them diligently unto your children, and shall talk of them when you sit in your house, and when you walk by the way, and when you lie down, and when you rise ...And when your son asks you in time to come, saying, What mean the testimonies, and the statutes, and the judgments, which the LORD *our God has commanded you? Then you shall say unto your son, We were Pharaoh's bondmen in Egypt, and the* LORD *brought us out of Egypt with a mighty hand...And it shall be our righteousness* if we observe to do all these commandments *before the* LORD *our God, as He has commanded us.*

God took Israel out of Egypt—from slavery—out of the customs of the world around them and revealed His law to them. He does not want His people going back to the traditions, customs, and ways from which He has called them out.

When people follow all the interconnected traditions, filled with the symbolism of worshipping ancient paganism and humanly devised gods, they are not worshipping the true Creator. Choose today to move forward and receive such a great gift and understanding of who and what you are.

Epilogue

Personal Reflection

Perception can be colored by one's state of frailty or state of power. In this move to Utah, I have experienced excitement and victory as well as depression and apostasy. Seeking and looking for that right moment; waiting for a sign or some type of relief from the pressure that I've felt within my inner being; wanting to be delivered, however, not asking but thinking and hoping. I have been left bereft, wondering if hope has left once again as before, wondering what is keeping me bound in a life of desperation despite that I know that Jesus is my Shepherd and I shall not want.

As I recalled the first verse of the 23rd Psalm, I could almost feel and hear the desperation in King David's prayer as he assures himself that the All-Knowing Deity has rescued and delivered him each time he has called. Even my mere thought of the God of Abraham, the God of Isaac, and the God of Jacob reminded me that I am endowed into a lineage of suffering and pleasure, blessings and curses, righteousness and iniquity, pitfalls and victory. My God of all, the creator of the heavens and the earth, the God of all things whether good or bad— He is God! I fell to wonder within myself if I have been the one destined for sufferings, heartaches, and disappointments that express the beast that

Personal Reflection

is in me or have I learned to suffer so I may obtain Christ Jesus, my hope of glory.

As I pondered this thought, as it wrangled itself into my concept of whom and what Christ is to me within my members, I cried out. I cried out the more, the harder, the sincerest, thirsting for water as the deer pants for the cool waters of a brook. I cried out, "Jesus, I need thee for I am broken and needed healing; teach me, fill me with You the more for I know that You can heal me." Was this truly my perception, the thought of one's destruction, or want? Where does one go from here? Do you continue to seek, to need, to desire a closer walk with Christ; to hear the sweet voice of your Savior, Jesus the Christ, say, "I am here, I have not forsaken or left you alone. I have not passed you by."

As I further struggled with this perception of need, I became aware of how I have sunk into the depths of the abyss I realized how, in the last seven years, I have become a bombardment upon the very essence of who and what Christ is in my life. In knowing numerology, I understood that seven means complete, thus I understood that during my test of torment, I needed to fully commit and submit to the awesomeness and love of God. I laid there waiting for the death of my flesh, a state caused by my tears of failures, my stresses of not meeting the mark, my lack of success. Would I be able to cause this beast to conform to the image of Jesus or had Christ already taken my brokenness and formed me into the very representative He so desires? The crying, the yearning, the hoping, and the desiring seemed to be lost during this season.

The physical pain of despair and oppression had seeped into the very thought of who and what I had become. Faith seemed to be a struggle of perseverance, hope became a mere thought, confidence had permeated into a shadow of what it used to be. My focus cloudily rested in the bosom of despondency. Even in this state of apostasy working within the confines of my ability, every blow from the enemy was life-threatening. As I recognized my joy was gone, every avenue of the ministry seemed to exist to destroy the very God that rested, ruled and was vested in me. My walk of Christ was attacked by the elders, titled people, and laypeople flaunting their positions of greed and self-want who were bound in the hell of Satan themselves.

I did traverse and arrive out of my valley of despondency. Knowing the path, I've now shared in these very pages, I encourage you to walk faithfully in the destiny God has prepared for you on.? By faith, you can achieve all that God has for in store for you I encourage you to do the same as me, which was letting all that I have gone through, all that I have been taught and driven unto me, to direct me to the Hope of Glory which is Jesus Christ.

I surmise that this journey leads me to my third book, Broken but not Destroyed.

As I reach the end of this book and the prelude to my next endeavor of authorship (my third book, *Broken but not Destroyed*), I want to leave with you not the abundance of knowledge and awareness, but the answer to the question, 'How can I escape?" If nothing else, know that Jesus, the First and the Last, is the answer for today. Now, try God Almighty, the Great I AM.

References

"3614. Oikia." Strong's Greek: 3614. οἰκία (oikia) — a house, dwelling. Bible Hub, 2020. https://biblehub.com/greek/3614.htm.

"Abstinence." The Free Dictionary. Farlex. Accessed June 29, 2020. https://www.thefreedictionary.com/abstinence.

"Addict." In *Encarta World English Dictionary*. Reading: Microsoft, 2000.

Barcley, William. "God's Building." Tabletalk. Ligonier Ministries, July 8, 2019. https://tabletalkmagazine.com/posts/gods-building-2019-07/.

"Beset." The Free Dictionary. Farlex, 2020. https://www.thefreedictionary.com/beset.

"Besetting Sin." Merriam-Webster. Merriam-Webster, 2020. https://www.merriam-webster.com/dictionary/besetting sin.

Bilson, Vic. "The Nature of Man." Jeremiah Project. Jeremiah Project, March 31, 2020. https://www.jeremiahproject.com/world-views/the-nature-of-man/.

Bluemel, Craig. *"The Violent."* 'The Violent'- The Kingdom of heaven suffers "violence". The Bible Answer Stand Ministry, 2007. http://www.bibleanswerstand.org/violent.htm.

Breitman, George. *Malcolm X, by Any, Means Necessary*. New York, NY: Pathfinder Press, 1971.

Cartwright, Mark. "Scylla and Charybdis." Ancient History Encyclopedia. Ancient History Encyclopedia, June 28, 2020. https://www.ancient.eu/Scylla_and_Charybdis/.

"Christianity." Encyclopedia Britannica. Encyclopedia Britannica, Inc. Accessed June 29, 2020. https://www.britannica.com/.

Clayton, Jonathan. Ms. *The Conceptual Worlds of Milton and Goethe*. New York City, 2012. https://academicworks.cuny.edu/cgi/viewcontent.cgi?article=1249&context=cc_etds_theses.

Driver, S. R., and A. F. Kirkpatrick. *The Cambridge Bible for Schools and Colleges*. Cambridge: The University Press, 1900.

Durant, Will. *The Story of Civilization. a History of Civilization in Italy from 1304-1576 A.D*. New York: Simon and Schuster, 1953.

"Flesh." Merriam-Webster. Merriam-Webster. Accessed June 29, 2020. https://www.merriam-webster.com/dictionary/flesh.

"Forgive." Dictionary.com. Dictionary.com, 2020. https://www.dictionary.com/browse/forgive.

"G1–Alpha–Strong's Greek Lexicon (KJV)." Blue Letter Bible. Blue Letter Bible, 2020. https://www.blueletterbible.org/lang/lexicon/lexicon.cfm?t=kjv.

Gaines, Janet Howes. "How Bad Was Jezebel?" Biblical Archaeology Society, November 11, 2019. https://www.biblicalarchaeology.org/daily/people-cultures-in-the-bible/people-in-the-bible/how-bad-was-jezebel/.

Gibbon, Edward, and H. R. Trevor-Roper. *The Decline and Fall of the Roman Empire*. London: David Campbell Publishers, 2000.

"Greek/Hebrew Definitions." Strong's #2889: kosmos–Greek/Hebrew Definitions–Bible Tools. Bible Tools, 2020. https://www.bibletools.org/index.cfm/fuseaction/Lexicon.show/ID/G2889/kosmos.htm.

"Grudging Definition and Meaning: Collins English Dictionary." Grudging definition and meaning | Collins English Dictionary. HarperCollins Publishers Ltd, 2020. https://www.collinsdictionary.com/us/dictionary/english/grudging.

Haaren, John H., and Addison B. Poland. *Famous Men of the Middle Ages*. S.l.: Dancing Unicorn Books, 2020.

Hewett, Caspar. "Auguste Comte – High Priest of Positivism." Auguste Comte–High Priest of Positivism. The Great Debate Home Page, 2008. http://www.thegreatdebate.org.uk/Comte1.html.

Hurlbut, Jesse Lyman. *Hurlbut's Story of the Christian Church*. Philadelphia: Winston, 1930.

Johnson, Paul. *History of Christianity*. New York City, NY: Simon & Schuster, 2008.

Knolles, Richard, Paul Rycaut, Edward Grimeston, Thomas Roe, and Roger Manley. *The Turkish History: from the Original of That Nation, to the Growth of the Ottoman Empire: with the Lives and Conquests of Their Princes and Emperors ... With a Continuation to This Present Year. MDCLXXXVII. Whereunto Is Added the Present State of the Ottoman Empire*. London: Printed for Tho. Basset, 1687.

"Lao Tzu Quotes." BrainyQuote. Xplore. Accessed June 29, 2020. https://www.brainyquote.com/authors/lao-tzu-quotes.

Larkin, Clarence. *Rightly Dividing the Word*. Philadelphia, PA: Moyer & Lotter, Printers, 1921.

Leiter, Brian. "Nietzsche's Moral and Political Philosophy." Internet Encyclopedia of Philosophy. Stanford Center for the Study of Language and Information, February 27, 2020. https://www.iep.utm.edu/nietzsch/.

Loughlin, James. "Pope Alexander VI." CATHOLIC ENCYCLOPEDIA: Pope Alexander VI, 1907. http://www.newadvent.org/cathen/01289a.htm.

"Malcolm X Quotes." QuoteHD, 2020. http://www.quotehd.com/quotes/malcolm-x-quote-we-do-not-condemn-the-preachers-as-an-individual-but-we-condemn.

Mansfield, M. F. *Royal Palaces and Parks of France*. Hamburg, Germany: Tredition GMBH, 2012.

Mickelson, Jonathan K. Strong James. *Mickelson Enhanced Strong's Dictionaries of the Greek and Hebrew Testaments: English ... Dictionaries of the Textus Receptus, the 1550 Step*. Atlanta, Georgia: Livingson Press, 2015.

Milton, John, David Aers, and Mary Ann Radzinowicz. *Paradise Lost*. Cambridge: Cambridge Univ. Press, 1974.

"Mortify Definition and Meaning–Bible Dictionary." Bible Study Tools. Salem Web Network, 2020. https://www.biblestudytools.com/dictionary/mortify/.

Nixon, C. E. V., and Barbara Saylor Rodgers. *In Praise of Later Roman Emperors: the Panegyrici Latini: Introduction, Translation, and Historical Commentary, with the Latin Text*

References

of R.A.B. Mynors. Berkeley, CA: University of California Press, 2015.

Nixon, C. E. V., and Barbara Saylor Rodgers. *In Praise of Later Roman Emperors: the Panegyrici Latini: Introduction, Translation, and Historical Commentary, with the Latin Text of R.A.B. Mynors.* Berkeley: University of California Press, 2015.

Riggenmann, Konrad Yona. "*Cruz e Criana: A Imagem Instrutiva Do Oeste Em 14 Estaes De Nazar Para Gaza.*" Google Books. BoD – Books on Demand, October 26, 2018. https://books.google.com/books?id=F9JyDwAAQBAJ.

Russell, Jeffrey Burton. *The Devil: Perceptions of Evil from Antiquity to Primitive Christianity.* Ithaca NY.: Cornell U.P., 1987.

Russell, Jeffrey Burton. *The Devil: Perceptions of Evil from Antiquity to Primitive Christianity.* Ithaca NY.: Cornell U.P., 1987.

"Skenoo Meaning in Bible–New Testament Greek Lexicon–New American Standard." Bible Study Tools. Salem Web Network, 2020. https://www.biblestudytools.com/lexicons/greek/nas/skenoo.html.

Slick, Matt. "Christian Apologetics & Research Ministry." CARM.org. Christian Apologetics & Research Ministry, October 5, 2017. https://carm.org/look-word-aionion.

Stewart, Melville Y. "The Greater-Good Defence: An Essay on the Rationality of Faith." Google Books. Springer, January 15, 1993. https://books.google.com/books?id=KTywCwAAQBAJ.

"Strong's #2663–Κατάπαυσις–Old & New Testament Greek Lexicon." StudyLight.org. StudyLight.org, 2020. https://www.studylight.org/lexicons/greek/2663.html.

"Strong's #3619–Οἰκοδομή–Old & New Testament Greek Lexicon." StudyLight.org. StudyLight.org, 2020. https://www.studylight.org/lexicons/greek/3619.html.

"Substance." Merriam-Webster. Merriam-Webster. Accessed June 29, 2020. https://www.merriam-webster.com/dictionary/substance.

"Subtle." Merriam-Webster. Merriam-Webster, 2020. https://www.merriam-webster.com/dictionary/subtle.

Szczesny, Mike. "[Greek] Ζυγός (Zygos), [Latin] Iugum." Resounding the Faith. Resounding the Faith, June 19, 2018. https://resoundingthefaith.com/2018/03/%E2%80%8Egreek-%CE%B6%CF%85%CE%B3%CF%8C%CF%82-zygos-latin-iugum/.

Thayer, Joseph Henry, Carl Ludwig Wilibald Grimm, and Christian Gottlob Wilke. *Thayer's Greek-English Lexicon of the New Testament: Coded with Strong's Concordance Numbers*. Peabody, MA: Hendrickson, 2017.

Topical Studies–Bible Tools. Accessed June 29, 2020. https://www.bibletools.org/index.cfm/fuseaction/Topical.default.

Webster, Noah. "A Dictionary of the English Language: Intended to Exhibi ...: in Two Volumes, Volume 1." Google Books. Black and Young, 1828. https://books.google.com/books?id=SBdFAAAAcAAJ.

"Your Vocabulary Building & Communication Training Center." respite–Definition of respite–online dictionary powered by

References

PowerVocabularyBuilder.com, 2007. https://vocabulary-vocabulary.com/dictionary/respite.php

CPSIA information can be obtained
at www.ICGtesting.com
Printed in the USA
LVHW021533110820
662923LV00013B/1252